Well, Shut My Mouth!

JOHN F. BLAIR, PUBLISHER
Winston-Salem, North Carolina

Well, Shut My Mouth!

The
Sweet Potatoes
Restaurant Cookbook

Cooking with Jazz!!

Stephanie Tyson

Stephanie L. Tyson

JOHN F. BLAIR
PUBLISHER
1406 Plaza Drive
Winston-Salem, North Carolina 27103

PHOTOGRAPHS BY SHERI CLAWSON
COVER DESIGN BY ANGELA HARWOOD
INTERIOR DESIGN BY DEBRA L. HAMPTON

Library of Congress Cataloging-in-Publication Data

Tyson, Stephanie L.
  Well, shut my mouth! : the Sweet Potatoes Restaurant cookbook / by Stephanie L. Tyson.
    p.   cm.
  Includes index.
   ISBN 978-0-89587-547-1 (alk. paper)—ISBN 978-0-89587-548-8 (ebook) 1. Cooking,
American—Southern style. 2. Cooking—North Carolina. 3. Sweet Potatoes Restaurant
(Winston-Salem, N.C.) I. Title.
  TX715.2.S68T97 2011
  641.5975—dc23
                            2011016720

This book is dedicated to the women in my life, starting with those five sisters—my grandmother and her four sisters—who lived their lives as strongly and with as much dignity as black folk, especially women, were allowed to in their time. They provided for their families in the tobacco factories and by being cooks, maids, and mothers in other houses in order to maintain the right to do so in their own homes.

This book is further dedicated to my mother. While not the best cook in the world, she provided my two brothers and me with enough food—and food for thought—for us to transcend our sometimes troubled existence.

This book is especially dedicated to Vivián—partner, editor, and friend—whose job it is to constantly keep my foot out of my mouth; to ensure that my clothes are properly buttoned, ironed, and matching; to taste stuff even if it has cooked tomatoes in it (which she hates); and to tell me honestly what she thinks (which *I* sometimes hate). It is Vivián who keeps Sweet Potatoes moving in the right direction as a business and as a citizen of the community. Without her, I would be lost.

Contents

Foreword

Our House
By Vivián Joiner

The intent was a space that would give a sense of comfort. Good friends, good conversation, and great food—an extension of our living room.

Welcome to our house, Sweet Potatoes, a restaurant born of a dream of being our own bosses, birthed from frustration at not being recognized for talent and commitment.

Stephanie and I grew up with very different experiences, she in Winston-Salem, the South of the sixties, and me in D.C., a world away. But some things were the same—family, food, and the fact that if we wanted something, we had to *work hard* to get it.

Sweet Potatoes grew from the lessons of our childhoods. Work for what you want. If you are going to do something, do your best. Those lessons gave us the example of working at jobs we may not have liked, but that provided the experience to take us to the next step in life.

We knew it would not be easy—and, believe me, not one phase of this journey has been. In the beginning, the banks turned us down for a loan (no surprise there). The city loan committee turned us down twice (a little surprise there). We were very busy from the first day (big surprise there). It seemed we had outgrown our space before we got started and needed to hire more staff. Stephanie and I both worked close to a hundred hours a week for most of the first year. Now, eight years in, we work a few less hours, but it is still seven days a week every week.

Our dream turned into sweet potato–colored walls with a splash of bright yellow sun. An aged mahogany bar and chairs. A staff of friendly faces that show the diversity sometimes otherwise invisible.

They may not always know the finer details of service or the French terms for cooking techniques, but our staff is a great bunch of people who enjoy food almost as much as we do. We have been blessed in that the people who come to our door looking for work have a real desire to be part of what Sweet Potatoes is—a place that feeds with a spirit of comfort.

Stephanie takes care of the food, and my job is to try to present it to our guests in a way that is worthy of the passion she puts into each menu item. Stephanie's passion for food and drive to do her best make those around her want to reach for the same bar. She dreams food. She enjoys the ability to feed, enjoys seeing others experience the communion that comes with preparing and consuming food.

People of different races, educations, and economic backgrounds can all relate to, if no other topic, food, whether the flavors of childhood or a new wondrous taste of Stephanie's South. To that end, my job is to sometimes be a taskmaster in the front of the house. Stephanie focuses on the food and the culinary staff, and I take care of the other staffing. I don't apologize for being hard on staff. You know the old saying, "You have only one chance to make a first impression." Well, we have only the next guest and the next plate that could send us out of business if we aren't on top of the little details. Everything we do is meant to make the meal an experience to remember—in a good way, of course.

You can't teach someone how to be Southern, but you can bring their Southern sense to the forefront. You can't teach being friendly, but you can remind people it's okay to take a moment to slow down and pay attention to those around them. Knowledge of what we do is a must for staff. Some former employees have told me that it's unfair to expect them to know the whole menu. Note that I did say *former*. Most of our regulars know the full menu, as well as past items. Sometimes, we hire people who have never worked, not because they are young but because they made other choices the first twenty-five or thirty-five years of their lives. We take those people and teach them basic skills that they can use wherever they decide to go when they move on from us. Our staff enjoys what Stephanie presents and feels an ownership about presenting it to guests.

My day may run as long as fifteen hours, but it's worth it. It normally starts with checking the reports from the previous day, then trying to keep up with all the bills. Much like at home, the day always seems to bring enough cash to pay most but not all of the bills.

Then it's time to open for the day by bringing the staff together for a "pep rally" and info session.

Uniforms are looking good.

Menu knowledge is good.

Everyone is ready to play host to a small Southern party at Sweet Potatoes.

I work the floor through the meal period, making sure folks don't wait too long for that first glass of tea and answering the frequent question of how and where green tomatoes grow.

When we were in the planning stage, Stephanie and I went around and around on what things should look like—what feel we wanted the space to have. Funny, how fate takes you where you should be. The space dictated many of the details, and money—or the lack of it—did much of the rest. What we ended up with was the combination of what we could do with the space and limited funds. The hand of fate gave us a beautiful bar and hardwood floors.

Our house—Sweet Potatoes—is that place we dreamed of. We do not have live music, but jazz is what you hear and feel when you come in. Jazz is America's music, born of soul and passion, feeding something deep within.

Our house—a place where you can be comfortable and at home.

Acknowledgments

I would like to thank God, from whom all blessings flow, for the people placed in my life.

And my grateful heart goes out to Philip Hanes, Lee and Myles Thompson, Shedrick Adams, Sheri, Tyra, Sharday, the terrific Sweet Potatoes staff, and our customers, who are without a doubt *the best*!

The commonality is the food.

Introduction

Our Story

How do you define Sweet Potatoes?

A super food filled with a day's supply of beta carotene, lots of Vitamin C, and potassium (I'm not sure it still has all that if you add sugar, butter, and eggs)

A really cool restaurant in Winston-Salem, North Carolina, that captures the flavors of the South with uptown funk and down-home soul to the beat of Ella and Miles

A place that employs a number of people trying to get back into the work force after making some mistakes and paying their dues—people who want and need to earn a living

A part of Winston-Salem and its growing arts community, with local artists adorning its walls, where any number of celebrities and noncelebrities can "get their feed on"

Vivián Joiner and me

All of the above

The name Sweet Potatoes just kind of came about. I like sweet potatoes. They're very versatile. I wrote the menu, and, looking over it, I said, "That's got a lot of sweet potatoes in it." I didn't realize it. So I said, "Oh, we'll call it Sweet Potatoes! That way, it can be like a running gag."

There's a folk-art painting that a woman, Currie Williams, did that's hanging at the wait station in the very back of the restaurant. Three weeks after we opened, we had our grand opening. Somewhere between the time we opened and the grand opening, she did this painting of us. I have a rolling pin in my hand, and it's going off the canvas. And the painting shows Vivián's hand, and she's holding a dollar bill.

So she had this painting in her studio, which was right across the street from us in a one-story building. She was going to present it to us. And somebody who had lunch at Sweet Potatoes walked across the street, went into the shop, and said, "Oh, that's Sweet Potatoes. I love that. How much is it?"

And she said, "Fifty dollars."

And the lady said, "If you add two hundred dollars to that, I'll buy it."

And so what does a starving artist do? She added two hundred dollars to the price, and the woman bought the painting. And in less than a week, she did another painting. We never saw the first one, but she told us, "I don't think this is as good as the first one." So we have the second painting. She's known as "the Apple Lady." All her paintings have an apple somewhere in them.

That painting is where we got the name of the restaurant. We had already decided we weren't going to have a big menu, so we had no space to tell our story. We wanted it at least to be "Sweet Potatoes—a restaurant." We didn't want it to be confused with a diner or a cafeteria, because when black people open a restaurant in the South, some folks assume it's going to be a cafeteria. "A restaurant" is in lowercase because it only states the obvious. We're just a restaurant. But there was also a restaurant in Hickory, North Carolina, called Sweet Potatoes, and it had already been trademarked, so we needed to change the name. That restaurant's closed now. I was in the wait station, and

Vivián and Stephanie as painted by Currie Williams, "the Apple Lady."

we were talking about needing to change the name. On the painting, it says, "Mmm Sweet Potato—Shut My Mouth," so we included "Well shut my mouth!!" in our trademark—Sweet Potatoes (well shut my mouth!!) a restaurant™.

. . . .

This book is recipes. Recipes from the restaurant, from my grandmother, from great-aunts, from Viviàn's mother and aunts and uncles. Recipes that are just Southern, plain and simple.

This book is about cooking and eating.

Although I'm as Southern as eating dirt, I have had the opportunity to see and experience how some of the rest of the world lives. Sweet Potatoes, and hopefully this book, are a reflection of that. Viviàn is from Washington, D.C., and has Southern sensibilities. Her father is from the Hilton Head area of South Carolina, so a few of our recipes have a Geechee flavor. My grandmother cooked for several white families, as well as her own family. I learned from her how to season food. My mother was part of the generation of increasingly liberated working women who had to come up with shortcuts to feeding the family—"out of the can and into the pan." I subsequently went to culinary school to pay a lot of money to learn that the thing that makes gravy thick is called a roux. In creating the recipes for Sweet Potatoes, I use all of those connections. Every part of me is a part of Sweet Potatoes.

The interesting thing about being the chef and co-owner of a fairly successful, albeit small, restaurant is that someone will invariably suggest you write a cookbook. My thinking on that subject was that there are already a lot of cookbooks. I know. I buy them all the time. I have hundreds of them. The best ones are those that are dog-eared and stained with flour and tomato sauce or whatever ingredients you put together for last night's dinner. My other thoughts were that I don't have anything *new* to say, and that I'm kind of busy, being the chef and co-owner of a fairly successful restaurant.

But something changed my mind. When I was growing up in Winston-Salem, my grandmother Ora Porter, who was the best cook I knew, gave me hope. She did not read or write well. As with so many

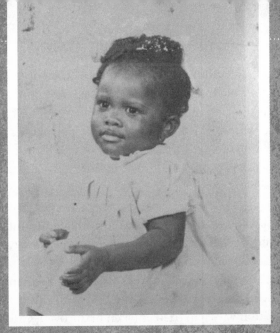

Stephanie, age one

The great aunts (left to right): Adele Joyner, Annie McCracken, Lizzie Carter, and my grandmother, Ora Porter. Ada Curry is not pictured.

grandmothers, everything she cooked was a pinch of this and a pinch of that. Her four older sisters—Ada, Lizzie, Adele, and Annie—were the same. But they fed me. And I have not forgotten. It was not easy watching the people you love and admire subjugate themselves for you. Some marched or did the sit-ins and made the six o'clock news. Then there was everyone else. They didn't invent the struggle, they just quietly went through it. That should be noted by someone every now and then.

My two brothers and I were latchkey kids. Our mom, Donzella, worked, so she cooked really fast stuff. And on one day every week, she would not cook at all. She said, "I do not cook on Saturdays. You're on your own." So that was when we'd go to our grandmother's house.

My grandmother always had something on—like a pot of butter beans. And she always had fried chicken in the oven. I don't know why we didn't get sick, because it was always in the oven, being warmed by the pilot light. We'd be over there like clockwork, at least once a week. And we always ate there on holidays.

When I got big enough, she'd let me peel potatoes—with a peeler, not a knife. She said I wasted too many potatoes with a knife. I thought it was so cool that she could cut up stuff in her hand and not cut herself, like chopping eggs with a really sharp knife. I wanted to do that. And then we'd taste. She'd taste, and I'd taste.

But it was never my intent to open a restaurant or cook. *Theatre!* I was Broadway-bound, by way of the East Carolina University Drama Department and the American Academy of Dramatic Arts in New York. This was a particularly daring dream for an awkward, shy black girl with child-bearing hips (somebody actually told me that when I was thirteen) from Winston-Salem. I had absolutely no experience. I had a speech impediment—a bad lisp. So it was kind of a surprise for anyone who knew me, that I would go into the theatre. But it was actually the place where I emerged. It brought me out of my shell.

I was at East Carolina about two and a half years before I decided to audition for the American Academy in New York. I was among thousands of other aspiring actors. I did musicals. I did a bus-and-truck tour of the Southeast. We stopped in Winston-Salem. My mom came and saw us at one of the restaurants where we performed. I did basic stuff like summer-stock productions of *Showboat*. But at some point, you can only play this Queenie person for one summer, and then it starts to get a little irritating, wearing that rag on your head.

Then I got to go to Europe with a production at a theatre festival in Vienna. And I stayed there longer than I was supposed to, because I did some nightclub stuff and a little singing. Then I auditioned for the American Institute of Musical Studies in Austria. But I wasn't really dedicated enough to do opera. I just learned a couple of arias for the audition, and that was it. I eventually came back to New York, but it was a disaster. If you can't take the rejection and that kind of pace, a little Southern girl just need not be up there. But I gave it a shot. Alas, as the song title says, "There's a Broken Heart for Every Light on Broadway."

To the relief of New York and my family, after about seven years of toil, minor successes, and major failures, I returned home to . . . pout. Unfortunately, I needed to pout at a faster pace than was possible in Winston-Salem nearly thirty years ago. I had no idea what to do. My family members were factory workers. They worked for Hanes Hosiery at the time. But that was not for me. The opportunity presented itself to work in Washington, D.C. To the relief of Winston-Salem and my family, I left, vowing, "As God is my witness, I will never live in North Carolina again!"

I knew no one in D.C. I had no place to stay. I had absolutely no money—less than two hundred dollars. I had no clue. I stayed at a hotel. I had done a little bit of research, and the hotel was not exactly what it said in the brochure. It was a horrible place. I could afford it for a week, until I got a paycheck. Then I got a room in a boarding-house that was even worse. I was in the basement of a row house. I was there for probably six months when my mom and grandmother came up to visit. They did not say a word about my little room in the basement with no windows and my little, tiny black-and-white TV that I bought at the thrift store. They were so sweet. They stayed for the weekend, and when they went back home, my mom sent me a few hundred dollars with a note: "Why don't you find yourself an apartment?" I don't know where they got the money.

I was there for about a year before I met Vivián. We met in a bookstore, and we clicked pretty immediately. I was working for Xerox, making copies. I didn't know anyone except some of the people I worked with. At that point, we became fairly inseparable.

When Vivián and I met, neither of us had a clue as to what career path we wanted to take. I eventually figured the restaurant business was for me, since it was too late to be a neurosurgeon. I started waiting tables, because I had done that in New York, where it's almost part of your training as an actor. I went to bartending school and wasted money there. I got some bartending jobs. Eventually, I started getting front-of-the-house management stuff in restaurants. I was a vegetarian at the time. For the most part, I burnt everything I cooked.

My first night of managing, one guy in the kitchen blew up at me. And being a person with a temper, I blew up at him, too, and he walked out. So, it was like, "Now what?" I had to struggle through the night, and I was completely intimidated by the kitchen.

At that point, I thought I might try culinary school. I applied to study culinary arts at Baltimore International College. I did really well there. When you're older, you're focused, as opposed to blowing your parents' money. I actually got it. It was probably one of the best things I've ever done because it brought back my grandmother's cooking. It all started to click. That's where I became most comfortable, in the kitchen. I probably never would have realized that had I not gone to culinary school. I see the kids go now. It's very expensive, and they figure they're going to come out and become a celebrity chef. But it's actually hard work, and you really have to pay attention and apply yourself.

Vivián opted for the corporate route—retail management and eventually corporate restaurant management, where she had no experience. But management is management. First, she was a host at a restaurant where I was bartender-manager. She started waiting tables there, and she was horrible. I'd make all these drinks, and she'd drop the whole tray. So I'd make the drinks and carry them for her, so I wouldn't have to make them over again. But because she's so detail-oriented and meticulous, she was really good at restaurant management. So she went through the steps. You hit that glass ceiling as a woman. There's no place to go. But with no background, she worked her way to being the general manager at different large chains of fast-food restaurants and quick-service restaurants.

We traveled from one end of the country to the other and back—Virginia, South Carolina, Florida, Arizona, Maryland—purposely skipping North Carolina. What were we seeking? Success, I suppose. Vivian found a certain degree of this in the corporate world, but I was a little too temperamental for such structure and restraint. We kept hitting these roadblocks. It was racial, and we're women, so we came up against it. I follow the food. It didn't quite work out, because it really isn't about food in corporate restaurants. It's about bottom line. I was stoked about, "Oh, this is really great food," but they weren't into that. They wanted to know that you could manage the money.

We moved to Charleston because I was interested in that Low Country type of food. It was a very difficult time. I'd come into a restaurant and the guy would say, "We don't hire women." But I landed at a place that was all women, lucking out with Charleston Place. I had a better time than Vivián did. She ended up waiting tables when she couldn't even get a job at Wendy's as a shift manager. It was very closed for her. We could barely afford the rent. And that's why we moved to Key West.

We visited Key West and liked it and decided, "Okay, that's it. We're moving." We sold everything that we could and packed the rest into a little pull trailer. We barely had furniture—just what could fit in that trailer. We towed it with a Geo Prizm, which is not a good idea. We stayed in Key West for three years. That was probably the best place we've ever lived. Key West is expensive, so we worked hard. Vivián had three or four jobs at the same time. I had gotten some good experience, and I could pretty much pick and choose whatever kind of job I wanted. I got a lot of food knowledge in Key West. That was the start of wanting to be more creative and wanting to have more creative control. We worked hard, but we also had enough money, and we could taste the different flavors in the different styles of restaurants.

Then we went to Orlando, where Vivián was a manager at Planet Hollywood. She was making way more money than me. We stayed in Orlando for six months and then moved back to Key West. But the Planet Hollywood there was slowing down, so we decided to go west with that trailer.

We headed to Arizona. Another thing you don't want to do with a Prizm is pull a trailer all the way out west. The country is rather mountainous, but you don't realize that looking at a map. We were 123 miles east of Albuquerque when we came to what we thought was a big hill. The Prizm went slower and slower and slower. Where the transmission goes through the car at the gearshift, it was hot. So we pulled off and dropped the trailer right there. We let the car cool down for about twenty minutes, then we continued up the hill without the trailer—without everything we owned, with the exception of our passports and birth certificates. Fortunately, we got to the crest of the hill and saw a town. Those people were really cool. They went back and got the trailer. We unpacked the trailer and put our stuff in a small truck, and Vivián drove the truck while I drove the car. The U-Haul place said we were lucky we didn't try to go up that mile-high mountain.

We went to Phoenix, where Vivián had a management position with Red Robin. Vivián always went for the living, and I always went for the food. I ended up at a country club, which turned out to be a really good experience. I had freedom there. I got a lot of catering experience, doing banquets and making food for five hundred. It was only two or three of us, so it was a lot of hands-on. They got me through a temp company. They liked me and wanted me to work there permanently, but they didn't want to pay the finder's fee, so they hid me when the temp company would come. "No, no, she's not here. We haven't seen her."

We were happy to get back to the East Coast. Red Robin was opening a restaurant in Maryland, so we ended up back near where we started. They paid for the move. But coming back was no picnic. It did not go well at all in Maryland. I was just sitting in the kitchen one day and said, "It's time to go home. I want to go home." And in fifteen years, I had never mentioned I would consider it.

By then, I had been blessed with the opportunity to work with different cuisines—Mediterranean, Italian, classic French—in varied venues like hotels, country clubs, private catering companies. But I never had the chance to cook what I grew up eating. My attachment to my grandmother's apron strings and soup pot had finally sunk in.

I loved food, especially her food—Southern food. And Vivián had hit that glass ceiling. My parents and grandmother were getting older, and so was I. It was time for me to come home. Vivián, as my copilot, came with me.

That was the best thing, because where we were, we would never have had the opportunity to open a restaurant. We were barely making a living and paying the rent. But coming back here, after living in an apartment for six months, you can own a house. Then you're looking at getting a business within a year of being here.

We had been talking for a few years about possibly—maybe, perhaps—opening a restaurant. The ability to control and create was very important to us. We came to Winston-Salem with a plan. Vivián continued in corporate restaurant management, and I worked in various restaurants around town. Meanwhile, we tried to raise money and find the perfect space for a restaurant.

Well, we at least found the perfect space. When I was growing up, Winston-Salem had never struck me as a hip, cool kind of place. That's why I left. But in my absence, it had rounded out its edges. It had, among other things, created an Arts District. Trade Street was part of that.

Growing up, I was never allowed on Trade Street. My grandmother referred to it as "the buzzard roost." It was pretty seedy. But now, what a difference! The space that we found was in need of a lot of work (a *lot* of work), but we had a vision of what it could become. Trade Street had blossomed into a neighborhood of small shops, galleries, and artists' studios. But no restaurant! The opportunity seemed perfect—to us, anyway.

We saw this space on Trade Street. The building used to be a rooming house and pool hall. Our space was actually the pool hall. The building was for sale. It was all boarded up, and it had one of those handwritten For Sale signs on it. It said $149,900, and the number had a slash through it, and the new price was $139,000. It seemed like a reasonable dollar amount. And then we walked around the back of the building, and one part was just a pile of loose bricks that had fallen off. But we looked through a little piece of the window, and I said, "That's where I want our restaurant to be. We'll just keep an eye on it."

And sure enough, a couple of weeks later, a guy named Mike Coe, who owned Coe Electric & Plumbing, bought the building, and Vivián immediately got on the phone and introduced herself. And he said, "No, ma'am. I promised the neighborhood I wouldn't put any alcohol back down there because they had such a bad time with it."

Vivián said to him, "Just allow us a few minutes to see what we want to do."

And five minutes after we met him, he said okay.

We had a plan. We had the experience. But others had very little confidence in our ability to take on such a daunting task, especially since what we did not have was money. Restaurants are risky investments. It was not enough that we were tired of working for other people and had the desire to create fabulous food with a Southern accent. No, the banks and the city loan people were having none of that. What they suggested, in a very condescending manner, was that we open a hot dog or hamburger stand. Or, if we had to open a café, we might not want to be bothered with serving any kind of alcohol. That might be too much for us. Even the people who were supposed to loan money when everyone else would not weren't interested. They thought that the location we chose was too far off the beaten track and no one would find it.

We continued with our plan anyway. It's amazing what you can do with credit cards (something I would not recommend), begging, and the goodwill of the right people. The late Philip Hanes, who was the commissioner of cultural arts in Winston-Salem, was that person for us. Mr. Hanes had heard that two women wanted to open a restaurant in the Arts District. He wanted to help, not financially but with influence.

Now, I grew up in Winston-Salem, but I had no idea who this guy was. On the telephone, he sounded like someone who had stepped out of a Tennessee Williams play—grandly Southern and courtly. But Philip Hanes was someone who could get people to do anything. So, with his brand of Southern charm and Vivián's absolute tenacity, we were able to secure loans from the city and the Meade Willis Foundation Redevelopment Fund, an organization dedicated to the rebirth and growth of downtown. Yes, we finally had the go-ahead to live the

American Dream. We may have been debt-ridden, hypertensive entrepreneurs, but we were in complete control of our destinies. Or so we thought. Everything has a price.

We were the first restaurant in the Arts District. It was kind of neighborhoody, with little mom-and-pop shops across the street. Being the only restaurant had an advantage as well as a disadvantage, because you're it.

Construction of the restaurant took place in November/December 2002 during the iciest winter I can recall. Renovations are difficult at best, since contractors seem to be on some altered timetable that never is in tune with yours. It was even tougher because of the weather conditions. Subsequently, Vivián became a contractor's worst nightmare. She quit her job and was at the construction site *every day*. Vivián is like a dog with a bone. She managed to get the contractor on our calendar, period.

"What are you doing?" she'd ask him.

"Give us a break," he'd say. "We just got here."

"What is this? You didn't measure?" she'd ask, tape measure in hand.

I felt kind of sorry for the contractor, because she was on him like the plague. But we got open when we were supposed to open. They said it would take eight to ten weeks for construction, so that's what we were going to hold them to. And we opened in nine and a half weeks. If Vivián hadn't been there, we'd still be trying to open, I'm convinced of it.

We put an employment ad in the paper the latter part of December, and we did hiring right before Christmas. Right after New Year's, we got our final inspections and finished hiring. The contractor still had his punch list to get done, and the health inspector had to visit. We did full-fledged training. We finally got our permission to cook. We would do a little bit every day, and I would adjust some of the menu items, but the menu was already printed, so it had to work. I was cooking, everyone was tasting, and we were trying to get the front of the house set up.

We were a week away from our projected opening day. Our plan was to open with no announcement—just unlock the door. We had staff in place, and while the kitchen had not actually prepared the entire menu, I was fairly confident that with my being there in the mix, we could do it. Unfortunately, all things are not foreseeable. My father suddenly died the week we were supposed to open. Nothing could have prepared me for that. I had no backup plan—no time to grieve or make the necessary preparations and do the things expected of the eldest child. Sadly, I left that to others. We had to continue forward. My father was laid to rest, and Sweet Potatoes opened as scheduled.

It is very important never to lose sight of your intent. But it is equally important to never lose sight of your humanness. That was a lesson I learned the hard way.

We opened the doors in January 2003. We didn't do any kind of announcement. We didn't have any advertising money. Our first day was a Thursday. We said, "We'll just see what happens." The forecast was for freezing rain. We took the paper down off the windows, and at eleven o'clock, we opened. For some strange reason, we were busy. People just started coming in. We filled up for lunch. I wanted to make sure the kitchen was doing the right thing, so at the dinner hour, we still did the lunch menu, because we wanted to practice that. And that evening, it iced, cars froze over, and we wound up having to close a little early. But people came. And Friday, more people came. And Saturday and the next week, we were busy. We outgrew our space within weeks of opening.

In the beginning, nothing was written down—no recipes. Because of that, I was in the kitchen from open to close. Although we already had the menu printed, I had created much of it in my head and didn't know if it would actually work, which is not the best way to approach menu development. Many of the items that I wanted to do were based on the food I grew up eating, but I had to create the recipes from memory. Eventually, after many trials and preparing a lot of food—including a few things that just didn't work—we developed a consistent way of doing things.

Although the handful of people in the kitchen were all at different skill levels, everyone started on an even playing field. We developed a policy of how our kitchen was to function. What I expect from people is respect for the kitchen and what we do. A professional appearance is important. We have tried to hire people of diverse backgrounds, including many who have come to us from prison. Everyone deserves a chance to earn a living and move on. But no sagging-below-the-butt pants—or the attitude that goes with it—in my kitchen. I insist on respect for the food and each other. Food is king, but good service is his queen.

We've been very fortunate with employees. One of our people, Fred Harden, was a little, hard knot from the moment he waited outside for Vivián to come and interview him. He waited there for a long time. He had just gotten out of prison. We hired him to wash dishes. He's still here, as a bartender now. They call him "Mr. Sweet Potatoes." He tells people he's my nephew. He's really not, but that's okay. I fired him. He came back six months later. That's the one guy who's been here almost from the moment we opened until now.

We've had other people who've just gotten out of prison, and they had no experience. It's hard for them to get jobs. But we've never made that an issue. It's about, "What can you do? What are you willing to do? Are you doing what you were doing before you went to prison? You're not doing that anymore? Fine, we'll start all over again."

Whatever they want to do in a restaurant, they have the opportunity to learn how to do it here. We had one person who started out washing dishes, and he really wanted to cook, so he started to wait tables and cook both. Eventually, he left, and he's doing really well. We've had a lot of folks come through who made some really bad choices. They spent not six months but two, three, twelve, fifteen years in prison. They learned from that, and they realized that they don't want to go back. Some of them were multiple offenders. But something finally clicked in their minds, and they came to us looking for an opportunity, for someone to give them a chance. Vivián and I both firmly believe that your past is your past, and if you can move on from that, then it should not keep you from flourishing. We've had a few who were knuckleheads. Sometimes, it takes the wind out of our sails, but we do bounce back, and we don't let that one person ruin it for the next person who may come to our door.

Community is really important to us—people sitting and talking.

That's why we don't have TVs, so people can have conversations. Our goal has always been to create an atmosphere that is an extension of our living room—just way bigger. Music is the key to setting the mood. The tone of the food is jazz. Sweet Potatoes *is* jazz. Jazz is the most diverse music I know, and it really reflects the faces that inhabit Sweet Potatoes.

The National Black Theatre Festival was a huge surprise for us. A lot of the actors you see on TV are a part of the festival, so they end up coming to the restaurant. We were unprepared for the amount of business we got from that. We opened in January that first year, and the festival was in August. It was unbelievable. At dinner, one of the staff came in and said, "You know, there's a line going around our block."

I said, "There is not."

So I went outside and looked, and there was a line going around the block of people waiting to get into the restaurant. And I thought, *Where are those people going to sit? And oh, my God, I don't have enough food.* We got a delivery of something from someone every day, and I still had to go out between lunch and dinner to buy groceries. I worry every festival because we still don't have the space.

During the theatre festival, we look forward to seeing some of the same faces. If we're not in the restaurant when they get here, they're a little upset. It's almost like a family reunion.

We've had some famous and infamous people come into the restaurant, and we love that they seek us out because we're not a glitzy or glamorous "in spot" but because they want to be treated well—with food, some Southern charm, wicked jazz playing in the background, and a glass—or two—of something.

All our customers are great. They're very protective of the restaurant. If something's not right, and we're not here, we're more than likely going to hear about it. The staff knows that. Sometimes, I sit and watch. The host, she's hugging the guests, or Fred is going over to hang out with the mayor.

The first year we were open, it was busy at lunch, and one of my church members came in. She was sitting at a table, and another family—a white family—was at another table, and their three-year-old was

fussing. So the church grandmother walked up to the table and took the kid, and she's walking around with this child so the parents could eat. They didn't even know each other.

Or people are sitting at the bar, and they're sharing food. I'm thinking, "Do you two know each other? Do you know he doesn't have cooties?"

It always amazes me how the one thing that people have is food. They may be different politically, economically, socially, but they still have food in common. Some in Winston-Salem still hold to the old social traditions. You know what? This is 2011. What else you got? That attitude is old, I think.

. . . .

Here's the question: How do you have a love affair with a place?

You start by loving what it does. The thing that we here in the South have in common is food—fried green tomatoes, candied sweet potatoes, fried chicken. When we break bread together, the barriers are lowered for at least a moment, and all things seem possible. *That* is the art of eating Southern.

So, one day, I'm sitting at the bar (admittedly a common practice) and wondering why this guy is by himself. We are not a pickup joint by any means, but we *are* a place for meeting people. The commonality is the food. It's nothing for the person at the next table or barstool to ask, "Hey, what did you order?" And less strange still for that person to offer up a bite with words like, "This is fabulous. You have got to try it!" Friends have been made and relationships forged over a basket of Fried Green Tomatoes and Okra.

Come to find out, the guy was sitting at the bar because he had a hankering for V.V.'s Mamma's Meatloaf and didn't want to share.

How's that for a job well done?

Desserts

Mmm . . . mmm . . . well shut my mouth.

Desserts

My grandmother was ninety-three years old when she died, and to that day, she always ate dessert first. I'm thinking, *Not a bad idea*. So here are desserts first.

I am not a baker. When we opened the restaurant, my intention was to find someone to do desserts. Well, we couldn't actually afford that, so I incorporated desserts into my cooking scheme of keeping it simple. If it is more than three steps, I'm not doing it!

These are tasty and simple.

Banana Pudding

Basic Piecrust

Lemon Chess Pie

Pineapple-Coconut Pie

Cranberry Chess Pie

**Sweet Potato–Cranberry–Pecan Cake with
Brown Sugar and Bourbon Cream Cheese Icing**

Sweet Potato Pie

Bourbon Pecan Pie

Sour Cream Pound Cake

**Easiest Devil's Food Cake in the World with
Chocolate Cream Cheese Icing**

**Sweet Potato Bread Pudding with
Pecan Crunch Topping
(Things to Do with Leftover Sweet Potato Biscuits #1)**

**Sweet Potato Apple Charlotte
(Things to Do with Leftover Sweet Potato Biscuits #2)**

My grandmother, Ora Porter

Banana Pudding
Serves 8 to 10.

In the restaurant, we make these in individual serving cups. My grandmother would make me one individual serving in a big ole bowl (which explains my hips)!

2 eggs
2 egg yolks
1 cup sugar
2 tablespoons flour
2 cups whole milk
2 tablespoons butter
1 tablespoon vanilla extract
approximately 1 pound ripe bananas, peeled and sliced
Vanilla Cookies (recipe below)
whipped cream

In a medium-sized bowl, beat the eggs and yolks well and add the sugar and flour. Pour in the milk and place over a pan of boiling water; the pan should be just wide enough to hold the bowl without its being submerged in the water. Cook for 20 minutes, stirring constantly, until the pudding starts to thicken. Remove from heat and stir in the butter and vanilla extract. In a 9-by-13-inch casserole (or your favorite bowl), layer sliced bananas. Top with Vanilla Cookies. Repeat for an additional 2 layers, ending in a layer of bananas. Pour the pudding over the bananas and wafers, then top with a final layer of cookies. Chill and top with whipped cream.

Vanilla Cookies

⅓ cup butter
1 cup sugar
1 large egg, beaten
¼ cup milk
1 tablespoon vanilla extract
2 teaspoons almond extract
½ teaspoon salt
2 cups flour
2 teaspoons baking powder

Cream the butter and sugar. Stir in the beaten egg and milk. Stir in the vanilla and almond extracts and the salt. In a separate bowl, sift the flour and baking powder. Add the dry ingredients to the wet mix until smooth. Refrigerate for ½ hour.

Roll dough into small balls (1 teaspoon) and place about 2 inches apart on a greased sheet tray. Bake at 350 degrees for about 10 minutes or until cookies are lightly browned. Remove to a wire rack and allow to cool.

Basic Piecrust
Makes one 9-inch piecrust.

A good sandwich starts with good bread, and a good pie starts with a good crust. It is the rarest of occasions when I make piecrusts. I just don't have "the touch" for rolling out good crusts. If you find that you, too, don't have "the touch," buy the piecrust. For the recipes in this book, store-bought crusts work very well. But if you've a mind to, and you think you have "the touch," this is a great recipe.

1¼ cups all-purpose flour
½ teaspoon salt
4 tablespoons cold shortening (lard actually works best)
3 tablespoons cold unsalted butter
4 or 5 tablespoons buttermilk

Blend the flour and salt in a medium mixing bowl. With a pastry cutter or a fork, mix in the shortening or lard and the butter until it resembles coarse crumbs. Add the buttermilk 1 tablespoon at a time, tossing the mixture with a fork until the dough comes together enough to form into a ball. Flatten the dough into a 1-inch-thick circle, wrap it in plastic wrap, and refrigerate for at least 1 hour.

Roll the dough out into an 11-inch circle on a lightly floured surface. Fold it in half and gently place it in a 9-inch pie pan. Unfold the dough and press it into the pan. Trim the excess pastry, leaving about ½ inch. Fold the dough under to form a high rim, then make a decorative edge. Fill the piecrust and bake as directed for the recipe.

Lemon Chess Pie
Makes one 9-inch pie.

Chess pies are the simplest of Southern pies—eggs, butter, sugar, usually cornmeal and/or flour. Lots of theories explain why they are called chess pies. One says they are a variation of cheese pie from England. Another claims they got their name because they held well in pie safes or pie chests. Either way, they are simply delicious—which is probably why they were kept in safes!

4 eggs
1½ cups sugar
1 tablespoon yellow cornmeal
1 tablespoon flour
½ teaspoon salt
⅓ cup melted butter
⅓ cup lemon juice
½ cup buttermilk
1 tablespoon lemon extract
1 teaspoon vanilla extract
pinch of nutmeg
unbaked 9-inch piecrust

Beat eggs in a mixing bowl. Add 1 at a time the sugar, cornmeal, flour, salt, butter, lemon juice, and buttermilk, mixing well after each addition. Stir in the lemon extract, vanilla extract, and nutmeg. Pour into crust and bake at 350 degrees until color is golden brown and center is slightly loose. Allow to cool before cutting.

Pineapple-Coconut Pie
Makes one 9-inch pie.

This version of chess pie is quick and delicious! My grandmother made these as small tarts. This recipe yields about a dozen 3-inch tarts.

4 eggs
1½ cups sugar
½ cup softened butter
2 tablespoons flour
8-ounce can crushed pineapple, including juice
1 cup sweetened coconut
1 tablespoon vanilla extract
1 unbaked 9-inch deep-dish pie shell

Beat the eggs in a medium mixing bowl. Mix in the sugar, butter, and flour. Stir in the pineapple, coconut, and vanilla extract. Pour mix into the pie shell and bake in a preheated 350-degree oven for 25 to 30 minutes. The pie should be golden brown, and the center should be set.

Cranberry Chess Pie
Makes one 9-inch pie.

Another variation of the same pie, this is a great dessert in fall, when fresh cranberries are plentiful.

½ cup sugar
½ cup melted butter
3 eggs
¼ cup flour
¼ teaspoon salt
⅓ cup buttermilk
1 teaspoon vanilla extract
1 tablespoon orange liqueur
2 teaspoons orange zest
2 cups chopped fresh cranberries
9-inch pie shell

In the bowl of an electric mixer set on medium speed, cream the sugar and butter. Beat in the eggs 1 at a time. Stir in the flour and salt, then add the buttermilk, vanilla extract, orange liqueur, and orange zest, mixing well. Fold in the cranberries. To prevent the crust from being soggy, prick the bottom of the pie shell and bake in a 400-degree oven for 10 minutes before adding the filling. Pour the filling into the par-baked pie shell and bake for 45 to 50 minutes in a preheated 375-degree oven. The pie should be lightly browned and firm.

Sweet Potato–Cranberry–Pecan Cake with Brown Sugar and Bourbon Cream Cheese Icing
Makes one 10-inch layer cake.

Somebody gave me a pumpkin cake recipe when we opened the restaurant, figuring I'd adapt it for sweet potatoes because I'd mentioned (a lot) that I don't like pumpkin. Over the past few years, that Bundt cake has grown into this really great layer cake.

Sweet Potato–Cranberry–Pecan Cake

6 eggs
3 cups sugar
1½ cups extra-virgin olive oil
3 cups sifted flour
3 teaspoons baking soda
¾ teaspoon salt
3 teaspoons ground cinnamon
¾ teaspoon ground nutmeg
¾ teaspoon ground ginger
3 cups baked, peeled, and mashed sweet potatoes
1½ cups dried cranberries (Craisins)
1½ cups chopped pecans
Brown Sugar and Bourbon Cream Cheese Icing (recipe on next page)

In a mixing bowl, add the eggs and sugar and beat at medium speed until smooth and light in color. With the mixer still running, slowly incorporate the olive oil. Combine the sifted flour, baking soda, salt, cinnamon, nutmeg, and ginger. Remove a scant ¼ cup of this flour mixture and set aside. Stir the remaining flour mixture into the egg mixture and beat at medium speed until well combined. Mix in the sweet potatoes. Toss the remaining flour mixture in a bowl with the cranberries and pecans to coat (this helps to prevent the cranberries and pecans from sinking to the bottom of the pan during baking). Fold the cranberries and pecans into the batter. Divide the batter into 2 lightly oiled and floured 10-inch baking pans and bake in a preheated 350-degree oven for 30 to 40 minutes until a toothpick inserted in the layers comes out clean. Allow cakes to cool in the pans for about 20 minutes, then remove from pans and cool completely before covering with Brown Sugar and Bourbon Cream Cheese Icing.

Brown Sugar and Bourbon Cream Cheese Icing

12 ounces softened cream cheese
1½ sticks softened unsalted butter
2 cups firmly packed brown sugar
2 tablespoons bourbon
½ cup finely chopped pecans

Combine all the ingredients except pecans and mix on medium speed until frosting is light and fluffy.

To assemble the cake, place 1 layer top side down on a serving platter. Spread layer with ⅓ of the frosting, place remaining layer top side up, and ice the top and sides with remaining frosting. Sprinkle with pecans.

Sweet Potato Pie
Makes two 9-inch pies.

You cannot have a restaurant called Sweet Potatoes *without an outstanding Sweet Potato Pie. For the most flavorful sweet potatoes, bake them, then peel and purée them. By boiling them, you will lose a lot of the flavor into the water, and the potatoes will be soggy. Try this recipe. We say it a lot: "No mamma slapping allowed!"*

2 cups cooked and mashed sweet potatoes
1 cup sugar
1 tablespoon flour
3 eggs, beaten
14-ounce can sweetened condensed milk
½ teaspoon ground cinnamon
½ teaspoon ground nutmeg
¼ cup melted butter
1 teaspoon vanilla extract
1 teaspoon lemon extract
¼ cup sugar (optional)
½ cup water (optional)
2 sliced sweet potatoes (optional)
2 unbaked 9-inch pie shells

Combine the mashed sweet potatoes with the sugar and flour. Stir in the beaten eggs. Mix in the sweetened condensed milk and add the cinnamon, nutmeg, butter, vanilla extract, and lemon extract, mixing well.

The following part is optional, but it looks really cool! Add the sugar and water to a saucepan. Bring to a simmer, add the sliced potatoes, and cook about 15 minutes until potatoes are barely tender. Allow potatoes to cool to the touch. Layer unbaked pie shells with sliced potatoes.

Evenly divide the sweet potato mixture between the 2 pie shells and bake in a preheated 350-degree oven for 45 minutes or until done. Pies should rise, and middles should no longer look shiny or wet.

Bourbon Pecan Pie
Makes one 9-inch pie.

Hmm . . . bourbon again. I'm sensing a theme.

3 eggs
½ cup firmly packed light brown sugar
¾ cup dark corn syrup
¼ cup softened butter
2 tablespoons flour
pinch of salt
1 teaspoon vanilla extract
1 tablespoon bourbon
1 cup chopped pecans
9-inch unbaked pie shell

Beat the eggs in a medium bowl. Add the brown sugar and corn syrup. Combine. Add the butter, flour, salt, vanilla extract, and bourbon. Mix until smooth, then fold in the pecans. Pour mixture into the unbaked pie shell and bake at 350 degrees for 25 to 30 minutes until the filling has risen and is no longer jiggly.

Sour Cream Pound Cake
Serves 8 to 10.

This is a very simple and good pound cake. I have been doing this pound cake for years. The base is always the same, but it's easy to change the flavor by adding lemon extract and lemon zest or almond extract instead. Topped with fresh strawberries and whipped cream, it is outstanding! The key to a good pound cake is having the dairy products at room temperature.

    3 sticks softened butter
    3 cups sugar
    6 eggs
    3 cups flour
    ½ teaspoon baking soda
    1 teaspoon vanilla extract
    2 teaspoons almond extract
    1 cup sour cream

Grease and flour a 10-inch tube pan. In a mixer, cream the butter and sugar. Add the eggs and mix until incorporated. Add the flour 1 cup at a time, mixing well after each addition. Add the baking soda, vanilla extract, almond extract, and sour cream. Mix to incorporate. Pour batter into the prepared pan and bake at 325 degrees for 1½ hours or until a toothpick inserted into the middle comes out clean. Allow to cool before removing from the pan.

Easiest Devil's Food Cake in the World with Chocolate Cream Cheese Icing

Makes one 9-inch layer cake.

Generally, if desserts involve more than three steps, I don't do them. That would make me a baker, which I am not. That's why I like this cake—everything in the bowl at once, mix, and bake.

Easiest Devil's Food Cake in the World

1½ cups flour
1¼ cups sugar
½ cup cocoa powder
1¼ teaspoons baking soda
1 cup buttermilk
⅔ cup oil
1 teaspoon vanilla extract
½ teaspoon almond extract
2 eggs

Place all the ingredients in a mixing bowl and mix on low until combined, then increase the speed to medium for another 2 to 3 minutes. Pour mixture into 2 greased, floured 9-inch cake pans and bake for ½ hour or until a toothpick inserted in the middle comes out clean. Allow cakes to cool.

Chocolate Cream Cheese Icing

3 ounces softened cream cheese
2 cups powdered sugar
1 cup semisweet chocolate chips
2 tablespoons butter
1 teaspoon vanilla extract
2 to 3 tablespoons milk

In a mixer on medium, combine the cream cheese and powdered sugar until light and fluffy. Melt the chocolate chips with the butter and allow to cool slightly before adding to the cream cheese mixture. Mix on low until smooth. Add the vanilla extract. Thin to a spreading consistency with the milk.

To assemble, place a cooled cake top side down on a cake plate. Spread ⅓ of the icing on the cake, top with the other layer top side up, and coat with the remaining frosting.

Sweet Potato Bread Pudding with Pecan Crunch Topping
(Things to Do with Leftover Sweet Potato Biscuits #1)
Serves 10.

I love Sweet Potato Biscuits. We use them for sandwiches at lunch as well as brunch. But what to do with the leftovers? The first thing I tried was this bread pudding.

Sweet Potato Bread Pudding

6 cups Sweet Potato Biscuits (see page 138), cubed
1 tablespoon almond extract
½ cup melted butter
2 cups sugar
4 eggs, beaten
1 tablespoon vanilla extract
2 cups milk
1 teaspoon ground cinnamon
1 teaspoon ground nutmeg
1 cup mashed sweet potatoes
Pecan Crunch Topping (recipe below)
Bourbon Caramel Sauce (recipe below)

Place the cubed biscuits in a buttered 9-by-13-inch baking dish. Combine the almond extract, melted butter, sugar, beaten eggs, vanilla extract, milk, cinnamon, nutmeg, and mashed sweet potatoes. Pour mixture over the bread cubes. Let sit for about 15 minutes to allow the liquid to soften the bread cubes. Bake at 350 degrees for 30 minutes or until just set. Remove pudding from the oven.

Spread the Pecan Crunch Topping evenly over the pudding. Return the pudding to the oven and bake for an additional 30 to 40 minutes. The pudding is done when it puffs up and a toothpick or knife inserted in the middle comes out clean. Allow to cool slightly before cutting into squares. Serve with Bourbon Caramel Sauce.

Pecan Crunch Topping

½ cup melted butter
2 eggs, beaten
½ cup flour
2 cups light brown sugar
2 cups chopped pecans

Combine ingredients in a bowl.

Bourbon Caramel Sauce

1 cup sugar
¼ cup water
½ teaspoon lemon juice
2 cups heavy cream
2 tablespoons bourbon

In a heavy saucepan, combine the sugar, water, and lemon juice. Cook for about 15 minutes until the sugar melts and caramelizes. Remove from heat and let stand for 5 minutes. Carefully whisk in the heavy cream, then add the bourbon.

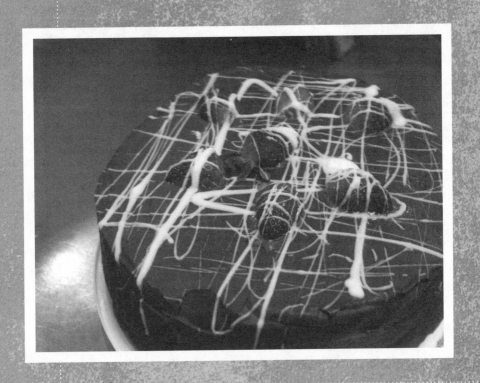

Sweet Potato Apple Charlotte
(Things to Do with Leftover Sweet Potato Biscuits #2)
Serves 6.

Charlottes are usually buttered bread, ladyfingers, or sponge cakes lined in a charlotte mold and filled with something—fruit or cream. I don't have a charlotte mold (I mean, really, who does?). This recipe uses Sweet Potato Biscuit crumbs—not ladyfingers, sponge cakes, or buttered bread. I probably shouldn't call it a charlotte at all, but I've already typed it.

4 cups Sweet Potato Biscuit crumbs (see page 138)
½ cup sugar
½ cup melted butter
8 cups peeled, cored, and sliced apples
2 cups brown sugar
1 teaspoon ground cinnamon
½ teaspoon ground nutmeg
1 teaspoon vanilla extract
6 tablespoons butter
powdered sugar for sprinkling
6 scoops vanilla ice cream

Combine the biscuit crumbs, sugar, and melted butter in a bowl. Divide all but about 1 cup among six 6-ounce ovenproof ramekins or individual charlotte molds. Press the crumbs on the bottoms and insides of the cups. Set aside, along with the reserved biscuit crumbs. Place the apples, brown sugar, spices, and vanilla extract in a medium saucepan. Bring to a boil, then reduce to a simmer. Cook for 15 to 20 minutes or until the apples are soft. Divide the fruit among the ramekins. Top with pieces of butter and cover with the reserved biscuit crumbs. Place the ramekins on a baking sheet and bake at 375 degrees for 25 to 30 minutes or until the charlottes are nicely browned. Allow the ramekins to cool enough for handling. Invert them on plates and gently remove the charlottes from the molds. Sprinkle with the powdered sugar and serve each with a scoop of vanilla ice cream.

Soups

When we break bread together,
the barriers are lowered for at least a moment
and all things seem possible.

Soups

soup (süp), *n.* 1. a liquid food with a meat, fish, or vegetable stock as a base and often containing pieces of solid food.

· · · · · · · · · ·

Yum! I'll have a bowl of that.

We do a different soup every day. Generally speaking, we just wing it. Soups are great because recipes tend to be only guidelines. I suggest being a little adventurous.

Basic Chicken Stock

Beef Stock

Vegetable Soup (Icebox Soup)

Tomato Basil Parmesan Soup

Gullah Gullah Stew

Chicken Mushroom Florentine

Savannah Crab Stew

Green Tomato, Chicken, and Sausage Gumbo

Quick and Easy Hoppin' John Soup

Callaloo

Basic Chicken Stock
Makes 4 quarts.

For the most part, we live in an instant world. You can buy perfectly suitable stocks and bases and make perfectly suitable soups from them. But given the opportunity and the time, make a stock—if for no other reason than that your house will smell fabulous! The stock can be frozen in small amounts in ice-cube trays.

1 onion, roughly chopped, skin included
2 celery stalks, roughly chopped, leaves included
2 unpeeled carrots, roughly diced
6 pounds chicken parts (backs, necks, and bones)
1 clove garlic
1 bouquet garni (4 bay leaves, 4 sprigs fresh thyme, ½ bunch parsley, all tied in a piece of cheesecloth)
6 quarts water

Place the vegetables, chicken, garlic, and bouquet garni in a large stockpot. Add water and bring to a boil. Reduce heat to a simmer. Occasionally skim surface of simmering stock to remove fat and scum. Simmer 1 to 2 hours, then strain and allow to cool.

This stock freezes well but should be left in the refrigerator only for 4 to 5 days.

Beef Stock
Makes 2 quarts.

4 pounds beef bones from your very considerate butcher
1 onion, chopped
2 celery stalks, chopped
2 unpeeled carrots, chopped
4 to 5 quarts water
beef scraps from your freezer
3 ounces tomato paste
1 bay leaf
½ teaspoon dried thyme
1 clove garlic
1 teaspoon black peppercorns
1 teaspoon salt

In a large roasting pan, roast the bones for 45 minutes to 1 hour or long enough to get some color. Halfway through the process, add the vegetables. Deglaze the pan with a little of the water to release the drippings. Add the vegetables, bones, beef scraps, tomato paste, bay leaf, thyme, garlic, peppercorns, remaining water, and salt to a stock-pot and simmer for 3 to 4 hours. Skim the scum from the surface. Strain. Refrigerate or freeze.

Vegetable Soup (Icebox Soup)
Serves a crowd.

My mother would be the first to tell you that she was queen of "out of the can, into the pan." But she did make one thing—vegetable soup, from all the leftover canned goods she froze. It was the best soup. This recipe really is a guideline. A word of warning: This soup takes on a life of its own and grows.

- 1 cup diced onion
- 2 cups diced carrots
- 1 cup diced celery
- 3 tablespoons vegetable oil
- 1 tablespoon chopped garlic
- 2 quarts beef, chicken, or vegetable stock
- 14.5-ounce can diced tomatoes
- 3 ounces tomato paste
- ½ head cabbage, chopped
- 3 cups fresh or frozen corn
- 2 cups green beans, peas, spinach, or anything else you have in the refrigerator, freezer, or pantry, including white and/or sweet potatoes

In a large stockpot, sauté the onions, carrots, and celery in oil until the onions are translucent. Add garlic and sauté 1 minute more. Add stock, tomatoes, tomato paste, and all other conjured ingredients and simmer until the vegetables are tender and the soup is thickened.

Tomato Basil Parmesan Soup
Serves 8 to 10.

This is probably one of our most popular soups! Think grilled pimento cheese sandwich.

1 cup diced onion
3 ounces tomato paste
2 tablespoons dried basil
1½ teaspoons chopped garlic
½ cup butter
¼ cup flour
3 14.5-ounce cans diced tomatoes including liquid
8 cups chicken or vegetable stock
½ cup heavy cream
1 cup shredded Parmesan cheese
2 tablespoons sugar
1 teaspoon white pepper
finely shredded fresh basil for garnish (optional)

In a stockpot, sauté the onions, tomato paste, basil, and garlic in butter until a smooth paste is formed. Add the flour and cook 1 minute more. Add the tomatoes and the stock. Simmer for 15 to 20 minutes. Purée the soup in batches in a food processor or using a hand-held submersible mixer. Strain the soup into a separate container to remove solids. Return soup to pot. Add the heavy cream and bring to a simmer. Add the Parmesan cheese and stir until the cheese has melted. Add the sugar and white pepper. Garnish with a chiffonade of fresh basil, if desired.

Gullah Gullah Stew
Serves 8.

This is a "Low Country state of mind" stew. You can experiment with ingredients—add shrimp, chicken, or more pork—or serve it with rice for a complete meal.

1 cup diced green pepper
1 cup diced yellow onion
¼ cup diced celery
½ cup diced country ham
1 tablespoon olive oil
1 tablespoon bacon grease
1½ teaspoons chopped garlic
1 teaspoon curry powder
2 pounds collard greens, washed and chopped
2 quarts Chicken Stock (see page 47)
½ pound frozen or fresh okra, sliced
14.5-ounce can diced tomatoes
15-ounce can black-eyed peas, rinsed
8-ounce can crabmeat

In a large pot, sauté the trinity (peppers, onions, and celery) and country ham in the oil and bacon grease for about 7 minutes till the vegetables are soft and the ham starts to brown. Add the garlic and curry powder and cook 1 minute more. Add the collard greens and Chicken Stock and bring to a simmer. Cook for 15 minutes or until the greens are tender, then add the okra, tomatoes, and black-eyed peas and cook an additional 10 minutes until the okra is tender. Add the crabmeat and cook to allow the flavors to blend and the crabmeat to heat through.

Chicken Mushroom Florentine
Makes 4 quarts.

8 boneless, skinless chicken breasts
salt and pepper to taste
1 medium onion, diced
4 celery stalks, diced, leaves included
1 tablespoon dried tarragon
2 teaspoons dried thyme
⅓ cup vegetable oil
1 teaspoon chopped garlic
2 pounds mushrooms, diced
½ cup flour
2 quarts Chicken Stock (see page 47)
4 cups firmly packed spinach, cleaned and clipped
1½ cups heavy cream
1 cup shredded Parmesan cheese
4 tablespoons cream sherry (optional)

Season the chicken breasts with salt and pepper and place on a sheet tray. Bake at 375 degrees for 15 minutes or until juice runs clear. While the chicken is roasting, sauté the onions, celery, tarragon, and thyme in the oil in a soup pot for about 5 minutes until the vegetables are soft. Add the garlic and mushrooms and cook an additional 5 minutes until the mushrooms release their liquid. Stir in the flour and lower the heat slowly. Add the Chicken Stock, stirring constantly. Bring to a simmer. Remove the chicken from the oven and allow to cool. Dice the chicken. Add the chicken and spinach and cook about 5 to 6 minutes until the spinach is tender and the soup starts to thicken. Add the heavy cream and continue to simmer. Add the Parmesan cheese and stir until the cheese has melted. Finish the soup with sherry, if desired.

55

Savannah Crab Stew
Makes 3 quarts.

½ cup diced onion
½ cup diced celery
½ cup melted butter
½ cup chopped garlic
¾ cup flour
1 quart clam juice
1 quart heavy cream
2 cups Parmesan cheese
1 tablespoon dried thyme
1 tablespoon Worcestershire sauce
½ cup dry sherry
½ teaspoon white pepper
1 pound crabmeat

In a large pot, sauté the onions and celery in the butter for about 5 minutes until the vegetables are soft. Add the garlic and cook 2 minutes more. Add the flour and stir till a smooth paste is formed. Slowly stir in the clam juice and bring to a boil. Add the heavy cream and lower heat to a simmer. Add the Parmesan cheese and stir until the cheese has melted. Add the remaining ingredients and cook for an additional 10 minutes to blend the flavors.

Green Tomato, Chicken, and Sausage Gumbo
Makes 4 quarts.

Green tomatoes give this gumbo a nice bite.

½ pound butter
1 cup flour
1 cup diced green pepper
1 cup diced yellow onion
½ cup diced celery
¼ cup vegetable oil
1 teaspoon chopped garlic
1 tablespoon Herbes de Provence
1 tablespoon Creole/Blackening Seasoning (see page 160)
2 cups diced smoked sausage such as andouille
2 cups diced cooked chicken
2 quarts strong Chicken Stock (see page 47)
3 cups medium-diced green tomatoes
3 cups sliced fresh or frozen okra
1 bay leaf

Melt the butter in a pan and add the flour. Cook on low heat about 30 minutes until roux is chocolate brown. In a soup pot, sauté the trinity (peppers, onions, and celery) in oil for about 10 minutes until vegetables are soft. Add the garlic, Herbes de Provence, Creole/Blackening Seasoning, and sausage and cook an additional 2 to 3 minutes. Add the chicken, Chicken Stock, green tomatoes, okra, and bay leaf and bring to a boil. Lower the heat and simmer for 20 minutes or until vegetables are soft. Add 1 cup of the cooled roux and cook an additional 20 minutes until the gumbo is thick and the flour taste is gone.

Quick and Easy Hoppin' John Soup
Makes 2 quarts.

½ cup diced celery
1 cup diced yellow onion
½ cup diced green pepper
1 tablespoon thyme
¼ teaspoon red pepper flakes
½ cup diced country ham
2 tablespoons bacon grease
1 teaspoon chopped garlic
2 15-ounce cans black-eyed peas
1 quart Chicken Stock (see page 47)
6-ounce package frozen collard greens
1½ cups canned diced tomatoes, drained
2 cups cooked rice

In a pot, sauté the celery, onions, green peppers, thyme, pepper flakes, and country ham in bacon grease for about 10 minutes until vegetables are soft. Add the garlic and cook 1 minute. Add the peas, stock, and greens. Bring to a boil, then reduce to a simmer for about 15 minutes. Stir in the tomatoes and rice and heat through. Adjust seasonings.

Callaloo
Serves 6.

If you serve this soup **on Sunday, it would be** *"Halleloo."*

4 strips bacon
1 onion, diced
1 tablespoon chopped garlic
1 teaspoon red pepper flakes
1 pound callaloo (spinach or collard greens may be substituted)
1 quart Chicken Stock (see page 47)
½ pound okra, sliced, or 10-ounce package frozen okra
16-ounce can crabmeat, picked for shells
13.5-ounce can coconut milk
salt and pepper to taste

In a pot, sauté the bacon until crisp; remove to the side and chop. Add the onions and sauté until translucent. Add the garlic and red pepper flakes. Cook for 1 minute. Add the greens, stock, and okra and cook for 15 minutes. Add the crabmeat and coconut milk. Season with salt and pepper. Garnish with the reserved chopped bacon.

Salads and Such

Community is really important to us—
people sitting and talking.

Salads and Such

When I was growing up, we didn't have a lot of salads—food before the food. Salad was lettuce or cooked greens like collards—it just depended on whose house you were at. Nowadays, everyone claims to be on a diet, and salad is their staple, no matter how much food is in it. My grandmother would eat a tossed salad, but it had to be simple, with iceberg lettuce, or she would say, "What's this? I'm not eating any grass."

Salads . . .

Down-Home 'Tata Salad

Marinated Crab and Potato Salad

Curried Chicken Salad

Tarragon Chicken Salad with Toasted Almonds

Green Tomato Carpaccio and Heirloom Tomato Salad

Black-Eyed Pea, Collard Green, and Tuna Salad

Stephanie's Salad (Junk Salad)

Summer Succotash Salad

. . . and Such

Butter Bean Hummus

Pimento Cheese

Hot Collard Green, Bacon, and Blue Cheese Dip

Carolina Crab Dip

Stephanie's Tomato Pie

Salads . . .

Down-Home 'Tata Salad
Serves 8 to 10.

Potato salad can be very tedious and time consuming. I make enough of the dressing so that I have to chop and dice only once and can have potato salad in short order. The dressing keeps for a couple of weeks refrigerated in an air-tight container. This dressing is also a quick and easy way to make Egg Salad (see page 144).

3 pounds white potatoes, peeled and diced
2 tablespoons salt
'Tata Salad Dressing (recipe below)
5 hard-cooked eggs, chopped
2 ounces diced pimentos, rinsed

In a large pot, add the potatoes, salt, and enough water to cover the potatoes by 4 inches. Bring to a boil and cook until the potatoes just start to soften. Remove from heat and allow to cool.

In a large mixing bowl, combine the potatoes and about 2 cups of the dressing. Add the eggs and pimentos and mix thoroughly.

'Tata Salad Dressing

2 cups mayonnaise
1 tablespoon yellow mustard
1¼ cups diced celery
1 cup diced yellow onion
½ cup pickle relish
½ teaspoon Texas Pete
1½ teaspoons granulated garlic
1½ teaspoons pepper
½ teaspoon salt

Combine all ingredients in a large bowl.

Marinated Crab and Potato Salad
Serves 4 to 6.

2 quarts diced and cooked red bliss potatoes
¾ cup diced onion
½ cup diced celery
¼ cup diced pimentos
1 teaspoon salt
1 teaspoon pepper
1 cup Dressing (recipe below)
½ pound lump crabmeat

In a large bowl, combine all the ingredients except crabmeat. Top salad with crabmeat.

Dressing

3 tablespoons lemon juice
1 tablespoon lemon zest
2 tablespoons white vinegar
2 tablespoons Dijon mustard
1 teaspoon chopped garlic
2 tablespoons dried tarragon
1 teaspoon dill
1 tablespoon sugar
1½ cups olive oil

In a small bowl, combine all the ingredients except oil. Slowly whisk in the oil.

Curried Chicken Salad
Serves 6 to 8.

This salad is big flavors. It is also a great way to use leftover chicken—turkey, too. Be sure to use a good-quality curry.

4 cups diced cooked chicken (combination of light and dark meats)
1 cup diced celery
½ cup diced onion
½ cup Craisins
¾ cup mayonnaise
1 tablespoon curry powder
1 teaspoon lime juice
½ teaspoon dried basil
pinch of cayenne pepper
¼ teaspoon salt
¼ teaspoon pepper
2 to 3 cups salad mix
¼ cup Major Grey's Chutney
toasted pecans or almonds for garnish

In a large bowl, combine the chicken, celery, onions, and Craisins. In a small bowl, mix together the mayonnaise, curry powder, lime juice, and basil. Add to the chicken mixture, along with the cayenne pepper, salt, and pepper. Mix well.

To serve, place the salad mix on a large platter and top with the chicken salad. Garnish with the chutney and pecans or almonds.

Tarragon Chicken Salad with Toasted Almonds
Serves 6 to 8.

4 cups cooked chicken (combination of white and dark meats)
1 cup mayonnaise
1 cup diced celery
½ cup diced onion
2 tablespoons fresh tarragon (or 1 tablespoon dried)
¼ cup pickle relish
½ teaspoon salt
½ teaspoon pepper
3 hard-cooked eggs, diced
¼ cup toasted almonds

In a large bowl, combine all the ingredients except the eggs and almonds. Fold in the eggs. Cover and refrigerate.

To serve, place the chicken salad on a bed of lettuce and top with the toasted almonds.

Green Tomato Carpaccio and Heirloom Tomato Salad
Serves 4 to 6.

Carpaccio usually consists of thinly sliced beef or fish in a marinade. Here, I use green tomatoes. This is a very colorful salad that makes great use of the bounty from the summer garden.

Green Tomato Carpaccio

¼ cup cider vinegar
2 tablespoons sugar
1 tablespoon pickling spice
1 pound green tomatoes, thinly sliced

In a nonreactive saucepan, combine the vinegar, sugar, and pickling spice and heat for about 5 minutes until the sugar dissolves. Pour the mixture over the green tomatoes and marinate for at least 1 hour.

Heirloom Tomato Salad

2 tablespoons cider vinegar
1 teaspoon sugar
¼ cup olive oil
2 pounds various heirloom tomatoes, cored and cut into bite-sized pieces
2 cucumbers, peeled, seeded, halved, and cut into ¼-inch half-moon slices
1 teaspoon chopped garlic
¼ cup rinsed capers
2 teaspoons fresh dill
2 tablespoons chopped fresh basil
2 tablespoons chopped garlic
whole basil leaves for garnish

Whisk together cider vinegar, sugar, and oil. Combine the remaining ingredients except for the whole basil leaves and toss with the cider vinegar mixture.

To assemble, place the green tomatoes in a single layer on a serving plate. Place the tomato salad in the middle. Garnish with the whole basil leaves.

Black-Eyed Pea, Collard Green, and Tuna Salad
Serves 6 to 8.

Somebody ought to be pleased. *This is a good-for-you salad. I mean, raw collard greens, for goodness' sake!*

2 15-ounce cans black-eyed peas, rinsed well
½ cup diced red onion
¼ cup diced celery
¼ cup diced green pepper
1 small cucumber, peeled, seeded, and diced
¼ teaspoon red pepper flakes
½ teaspoon chopped garlic
1 small bunch collard greens (about 2 cups), tough stems removed,
    cleaned, and finely chopped
10-ounce can white albacore tuna, drained
½ teaspoon salt
½ teaspoon pepper
¼ cup Key lime juice
¼ cup cider vinegar
1 tablespoon honey
½ cup extra-virgin olive oil
lime slices for garnish

In a large bowl, combine all the ingredients except for the last 5. In a small bowl, combine the Key lime juice, cider vinegar, and honey. Slowly whisk in the olive oil. Pour over the salad ingredients. Refrigerate for at least 2 hours before serving. Garnish with slices of lime.

Stephanie's Salad (Junk Salad)
Serves 8 to 10.

With pizza, I am one ingredient at a time. But I love lots of stuff on a salad! This is like a bowl of salad bar.

5 cups salad mix (assorted greens)
6 ounces canned corn
1 3.75-ounce can kidney beans, rinsed
1 cup diced beets, rinsed
1 red onion, sliced
1 cup diced cooked turkey and/or ham
1 cucumber, peeled, seeded, and diced
1 cup blanched green beans
¾ cup blue cheese, crumbled
Balsamic Vinaigrette (recipe below)
3 tomatoes, cut into wedges
½ cup shredded sweet potatoes
½ cup crispy potato sticks

In a large salad bowl, combine all the ingredients except for the tomatoes, sweet potatoes, and potato sticks. Garnish the bowl with the tomatoes and top with the shredded sweet potatoes and potato sticks.

Balsamic Vinaigrette
Makes about 3 cups.

½ cup Dijon mustard
¼ cup balsamic vinegar
3 tablespoons molasses
1½ teaspoons dried basil
1½ teaspoons pepper
1½ teaspoons chopped garlic
1½ teaspoons kosher salt
2 cups plus 2 tablespoons extra-virgin olive oil

Combine all the ingredients except for the oil. Using a hand-held immersion mixer, blend the ingredients and slowly add the oil until an emulsion has been formed.

Summer Succotash Salad
Serves 6 to 8.

This is another salad that makes great use of the summer garden.

1 pound fresh green beans, cut into 1½-inch pieces
2 cups fresh or frozen lima beans
1 sweet onion, diced
1 green pepper, diced
1 celery stalk, diced
3 or 4 ears fresh corn, cut from the cob (about 2 cups corn)
1 tablespoon olive oil
2 or 3 tomatoes, peeled and diced
Dressing (recipe below)
¼ cup chopped basil
1 tablespoon chopped fresh thyme or 1 teaspoon dried thyme
salt and pepper to taste

In a pot of boiling water, add the green beans and cook for 3 minutes or until just tender. Remove with a slotted spoon and shock in cold water. Add the lima beans to the pot of boiling water and cook for 4 minutes. Remove and allow to cool. Sauté the onions, green peppers, celery, and corn in the olive oil for 2 to 3 minutes. Remove from heat and allow to cool. Place the cooled vegetables and diced tomatoes in a large bowl and toss to combine. Stir in the Dressing. Fold in the chopped herbs. Season with salt and pepper. Serve chilled.

Dressing

¼ cup cider vinegar
2 tablespoons Dijon mustard
1 teaspoon sugar

½ cup olive oil
½ teaspoon salt
½ teaspoon pepper

In a medium bowl, combine the cider vinegar, Dijon mustard, and sugar. Slowly whip in the olive oil. Add the salt and pepper.

. . . and Such

Butter Bean Hummus
Makes 2 cups.

This is a very vegetarian-friendly recipe. But sometimes when I'm not feeling so friendly, I will use a combination of olive oil and bacon grease and garnish the hummus with country ham bits. Serve either version with toasted pita or Sweet Potato Biscuit chips (see page 138).

15-ounce can butter beans
2 tablespoons peanut butter
2 tablespoons fresh lemon juice
zest of 1 lemon
3 cloves garlic, crushed
1 teaspoon ground cumin
¼ teaspoon cayenne pepper
¼ teaspoon salt
¼ teaspoon white pepper
¼ cup olive oil

In the bowl of a food processor, combine all the ingredients except the olive oil. With the processor running, slowly add the olive oil. Refrigerate.

77

Pimento Cheese
Makes 4 cups.

A Southern classic.

2 cups mayonnaise
4-ounce package cream cheese
1½ tablespoons onion powder
1½ teaspoons granulated garlic
1¼ teaspoons paprika
pinch of cayenne pepper
¼ teaspoon salt
¼ teaspoon white pepper
½ teaspoon sugar
½ cup grated white cheddar cheese
2 cups grated yellow cheddar cheese
¾ cup diced pimentos, rinsed

Combine the mayonnaise and cream cheese in a mixer until smooth. Add the onion powder, garlic, paprika, cayenne, salt, white pepper, and sugar. Mix until combined, then fold in the cheeses until thoroughly incorporated. Stir in the pimentos.

Serving suggestion: Use as an elegant dip in your most festive dish with crudités, or use in a sandwich on white toast with a piece of perfectly charred fried bologna.

Hot Collard Green, Bacon, and Blue Cheese Dip
Makes 4 cups.

1 cup sour cream
½ cup Parmesan cheese, plus additional for garnish
½ cup crumbled blue cheese
¼ cup cream cheese
½ cup chopped cooked bacon
4 cups spicy greens or 2 14.5-ounce cans collard greens, rinsed
¼ cup diced pimentos
Texas Pete

In a large mixing bowl, combine the sour cream, ½ cup Parmesan cheese, blue cheese, cream cheese, and bacon. Drain the greens. Add the greens and pimentos. Finish with about 2 shakes of Texas Pete.

Spray or oil the inside of a 2-quart casserole dish. Add the dip and sprinkle with a little Parmesan cheese. Bake at 375 degrees for about 15 minutes until the dip is hot and bubbling.

Carolina Crab Dip
Makes 2 cups.

This cold dip is so easy it's almost embarrassing! Serve it with crackers or toast points.

1 pint crabmeat
½ cup sour cream
½ cup mayonnaise
1 tablespoon Old Bay seasoning
¼ cup chopped parsley
1 tablespoon dry sherry

Carefully pick through the crabmeat. An easy way is to spread the crabmeat on a sheet tray and place it under the broiler for 30 seconds to 1 minute. The heat will make the shells turn white, making it easier to see them.

e the sour cream, mayonnaise, Old Bay seasoning, pars-
rry. Fold in the crabmeat. Chill.

hie's Tomato Pie

Serves b.

9-inch pie shell
3 or 4 ripe tomatoes, peeled* and diced
¼ cup julienned fresh basil
1 or 2 green onions, chopped
2 teaspoons chopped fresh thyme
½ cup Parmesan cheese
1 teaspoon salt
1 teaspoon pepper
1 cup homemade Pimento Cheese (see page 78)

Bake the piecrust in a 350-degree oven for about 10 minutes until lightly browned. In a medium bowl, combine the diced tomatoes,
basil, green onions, thyme, and ½ of the Parmesan cheese. Add the
salt and pepper. Sprinkle the remaining Parmesan cheese on the bottom of the crust and layer with the tomato mixture. Spread evenly
with the Pimento Cheese. Bake for 30 to 45 minutes until bubbly and
brown. Serve warm or at room temperature.

*To easily peel the tomato, make an *X* with a shrimp knife on the
bottom of the tomato. Remove the core and drop it into the boiling
water for about 30 seconds. Remove and drop into ice water. The
skin should come off easily.

Meats
and
Yard Birds
(and Their Cousins)

It is very important to never
lose sight of your intent.
But it is equally important
to never lose sight
of your humanness.

Meats and Yard Birds
(and Their Cousins)

No one would ever guess that at one point in my life I was a vegetarian, because I love meat, especially pork. It's very versatile, much like chicken. I could write an ode to the pig. It's the thing you ate high off of when doing well and from other parts south when things were tough. Beef is perfect for braising to extract the most flavor. And chicken! I tell you, if I had been captain of Noah's Ark, there would have been two two-by-twos missing—Mr. Chicken, Miss Piggy, and their mates!

Drunken Pork Chops with Country Ham Bordelaise

Three Little Pigs
(Bacon-Wrapped Pork Loin Stuffed with Chopped BBQ Pork)

Cheerwine-Glazed Country Ham

Braised Pork Belly and Butter Bean Ragout

How to Fry a Chicken
(and Why I Think You Should, at Least on Sundays)

Buttermilk Fried Chicken

Miss Ora's Best Fried Chicken in the Entire World

Chicken Country Captain

Pan-Roasted Oyster-Stuffed Quail with Red-Eye Gravy

V. V.'s Mamma's Meatloaf with Wild Mushroom Gravy

Slow Cooker Chocolate Stout Pot Roast

Roasted Rack of Lamb with Mint Julep Sauce

Drunken Pork Chops with Country Ham Bordelaise
Serves 3 to 6.

Drunken Pork Chops

6 boneless thick-sliced pork chops
1 cup apple brandy or hard cider
2 teaspoons chopped garlic
½ teaspoon Herbes de Provence
½ cup vegetable oil
2 teaspoons kosher salt
pepper to taste

Combine all the ingredients except for the pepper in a nonreactive dish and allow to marinate for 4 hours or overnight.

Remove the pork chops from the marinade and season with pepper. In a large skillet or a grill pan, cook the pork chops about 6 minutes on each side. Serve with Country Ham Bordelaise (recipe below) and Sweet Potato Cornbread Stuffing (see page 127).

Country Ham Bordelaise
Makes 4 cups.

3 or 4 strips bacon
¾ cup diced country ham
½ cup diced yellow onion
¼ teaspoon dried thyme
¼ teaspoon dried sage
½ teaspoon chopped garlic
2 tablespoons apple brandy
½ cup red wine
3 cups beef stock
½ cup brown roux (see instructions under Green Tomato, Chicken, and Sausage Gumbo, page 58)
pepper to taste

In a medium saucepan, cook the bacon until crispy. Remove and crumble. Sauté the country ham, onions, thyme, and sage in the remaining bacon grease until onions begin to soften. Add the garlic and sauté 2 minutes more. Deglaze the pan with apple brandy. Add the red wine. Cook and reduce by ½. Add the beef stock and return to a simmer. Add the roux and cook for 10 minutes or until the flour taste has dissipated. Add pepper.

Three Little Pigs (Bacon-Wrapped Pork Loin Stuffed with Chopped BBQ Pork)
Serves 6.

This is a pork lover's dream!

1 small bunch collard greens
½ cup hot chicken broth
3-pound pork loin, butterflied
salt and pepper to taste
2 cups of your favorite chopped BBQ pork
7 or 8 strips applewood smoked bacon
BBQ Jus (recipe on next page)

Wash the collard greens, removing the tough ribs from the greens but leaving them as whole as possible. Blanch the greens in the hot chicken broth for about 10 minutes until they are tender. Remove and allow to cool.

Place the butterflied pork loin on a flat work surface. Season the loin liberally with salt and pepper. Line the loin with the collard greens, spreading the leaves as much as possible to create a thin layer. Spoon the BBQ down the middle of the greens and pork in a horizontal line. Roll the pork tightly, seam side down. Season with additional salt and pepper. Wrap the roll with the bacon strips so that the loin is covered. Tie tightly with butcher's twine and carefully place in a shallow roasting pan. Bake at 350 degrees for about 1 hour until the internal temperature reaches 150 degrees. Turn the temperature up to 400 degrees and roast for an additional 20 to 30 minutes to crisp

the bacon and allow the internal temperature to reach 160 degrees.
Allow the roast to cool before slicing. Serve with BBQ Jus.

BBQ Jus

1 tablespoon vegetable oil
½ cup chopped onion
4 tablespoons chopped garlic
1½ cups ketchup
2 tablespoons brown sugar
1½ teaspoons horseradish
2 tablespoons cider vinegar
1½ teaspoons chili powder
1½ teaspoons Texas Pete
¼ cup beef broth

In a small saucepan, add the oil and sauté the onions for about
4 minutes until soft. Add the remaining ingredients and simmer for
about 10 minutes.

Cheerwine-Glazed Country Ham
Serves 15 to 20.

I love country ham (versus city ham). You can get center-cut slices or pieces or prepare a whole ham. While very time consuming, the actual cooking process is relatively pain-free. Soaking the ham is the key. This helps to get rid of some (but not all) of the saltiness. And to help get you through the preparation, try a tall glass of frosty Cheerwine soda!

13- to 14-pound country ham
½ liter Cheerwine
1 cup apple cider vinegar
½ cup Dijon mustard
Glaze (recipe on next page)

Scrub the ham with a stiff brush under running water to remove excess cure and mold. Place the ham in a container large enough to hold it and fill with cold water. Soak for at least 2 days, changing the water daily.

After soaking, place the ham in a large roasting pan, skin side up. Combine the Cheerwine, cider vinegar, and Dijon mustard and pour over the ham. Cover or place foil over the pan. Place the roasting pan in an oven preheated to 325 degrees. Cook the ham about 20 to 25 minutes per pound (4 to 5 hours for a 14-pound ham) or until the internal temperature reaches 155 degrees. Allow the ham to cool. Remove to a flat surface and remove the rind. Trim some of the fat, leaving about ¼ inch of fat. Score the fat with a sharp knife, making diamond patterns.

Pour the Glaze over the ham and bake for 15 minutes. Check the ham to make sure it isn't getting too dark. Baste the ham with additional Glaze and bake for another 25 to 30 minutes or until the ham is nicely browned. Serve thinly sliced.

Serving suggestion: Try this ham with Down-Home 'Tata Salad (see page 65) and Spicy Greens (see page 124).

Glaze

the other ½ liter of Cheerwine
2 cups brown sugar
pinch of allspice

Combine all the ingredients in a medium bowl.

Braised Pork Belly and Butter Bean Ragout
Serves 4.

1½-pound pork belly
2 tablespoons Montreal Steak Seasoning
1 onion, chopped
2 celery stalks, chopped
2 carrots, peeled and chopped
2 cups diced tomatoes
4 cloves garlic, peeled
1 star anise
1 cup dry vermouth
6 to 8 cups chicken broth
2 cups dried butter beans
jar of your favorite chow-chow

Prepare the pork belly by trimming the fat to about ¼ inch. Cut slits in the fat, being careful not to cut into the meat. Rub the meat on all sides with Montreal Steak Seasoning. In a large, hot skillet, brown the belly on all sides. Place the vegetables, garlic, and star anise in a roasting pan. Remove the belly from the skillet and place on top of the vegetables. Deglaze the skillet with the dry vermouth and pour into the roasting pan, along with the chicken broth. Cover and place in a 325-degree oven for 1½ hours.

While the pork belly is roasting, add the butter beans to a large pot with enough water to cover beans by 4 inches. Bring the pot to a boil and cook for about ½ hour. Turn the pot off and let the beans sit covered for 1 hour.

Remove the roasting pan from the oven. Add the beans to the pan, cover, and put back into the oven for an additional 1½ hours or until the beans are done and the pork is fork tender.

Remove the pan from the oven and divide the pork belly into 4 equal portions. Serve on top of the butter beans. Serve each portion with 2 tablespoons of chow-chow.

How to Fry a Chicken (and Why I Think You Should, at Least on Sundays)

I eat a lot of chicken. The doctor says my cholesterol is high, my blood pressure is high, my weight is high. The only thing that is not high is my enthusiasm for what the doctor says.

Baked chicken, broiled chicken, grilled chicken. Chicken braised and stewed. But—gasp!—not fried! No more fried chicken. Can this be possible, a Southern gal such as me asked to turn her back on that cast-iron pan with oil bubbling and popping, filled with flour-coated legs, thighs, and a wing or two, the scent in the air?

Heck no! (Sorry, Doc.) And here's why. Tradition. Those traditions of lynchings and cross burnings are good ones to have lost. But sitting on the porch on a Sunday afternoon following church, saying "Yes, ma'am" and "Yes, sir" to anybody older than you, and frying chicken for supper—those types of traditions we need.

Frying chicken is no joke. It takes time and thought. My grand-mother fried chicken simply. She seasoned it with salt and pepper after she cleaned it (usually the day before she was going to cook it) and dredged it in flour that was seasoned with salt and pepper. And she fried it in grease that always had a piece of fatback in it. I got to eat the chicken and the piece of fatback. (I'm sure that has nothing to do with my cholesterol issue.) It was the best fried chicken I've ever had.

At Sweet Potatoes, we do Buttermilk Fried Chicken with a few more spices and, alas, no fatback. But it's still very tasty chicken. I've included recipes for both. But whatever method you choose, it doesn't matter—just fry the chicken!

Buttermilk Fried Chicken
Serves 4.

1 quart buttermilk
2 tablespoons kosher salt
1 teaspoon granulated garlic
1 teaspoon dried thyme
1 tablespoon pepper
2- to 3-pound chicken, cut up and cleaned
vegetable oil for frying
2 cups all-purpose flour
3 tablespoons cornstarch
2 tablespoons Chicken and Seafood Seasoning (see page 159)

Combine the buttermilk, salt, garlic, thyme, and pepper in a large bowl. Add the chicken. Cover and refrigerate for 6 hours or overnight.

Heat the oil in a large skillet or a cast-iron pan. Combine the flour, cornstarch, and Chicken and Seafood Seasoning in a bowl. Dredge the chicken in the flour mixture, coating it well. Add the chicken to the oil and brown on 1 side for about 10 minutes. Turn the chicken over and continue to fry. The chicken is done when an instant-read thermometer inserted in the thickest part registers 170 degrees.

Miss Ora's Best Fried Chicken in the Entire World
Serves 4.

3-pound fryer, cut up
salt and pepper to taste
2 cups flour
½ teaspoon salt
½ teaspoon pepper
vegetable oil for frying
3 or 4 slices fatback

Season the chicken with salt and pepper up to a day before frying.

Combine the flour, ½ teaspoon salt, and ½ teaspoon pepper in a resealable plastic bag. Add the chicken to the bag a few pieces at a time and shake to coat. Fill a pan ½ full with oil. Heat the oil. When the oil is hot, add the chicken and fatback, being careful not to crowd the pan. Fry the chicken till brown on 1 side, then turn and continue cooking until done. Remove and drain on paper towels. Eat the chicken. Eat the fatback.

Chicken Country Captain
Serves 4.

½ cup all-purpose flour
½ teaspoon salt
½ teaspoon pepper
2 teaspoons smoked paprika
3 strips bacon
4 chicken leg quarters, cut into legs and thighs
¼ cup vegetable oil
2 green peppers, diced
1 medium onion, diced
2 celery stalks, diced
1 teaspoon chopped garlic
1 tablespoon curry powder
14.5-ounce can diced tomatoes
1 cup chicken stock
½ cup dried cranberries
1 cup toasted chopped pecans
¼ cup chopped cilantro (optional)
4 cups cooked white rice

In a bowl, combine the flour, salt, pepper, and paprika. Cook the bacon in a large skillet until crisp. Remove, drain on a paper towel, and crumble. Dredge the chicken pieces in the flour mixture. Add the vegetable oil to the skillet. Add the chicken to the hot oil and cook about 8 minutes on each side until nicely browned. Remove the chicken to a large casserole dish. Place the peppers, onions, and celery in the skillet and sauté about 5 minutes until the onions are translucent. Add the garlic and curry powder and cook an additional 2 to 3 minutes or until the curry powder is fragrant. Add the tomatoes and chicken stock and bring to a simmer. Pour the sauce over the chicken and sprinkle the cranberries over the top. Cover the dish with foil, place in a 425-degree oven, and bake for 20 to 30 minutes until the chicken is done and the sauce has thickened. Uncover and top with the crumbled bacon and toasted pecans. Garnish with the chopped cilantro, if desired, and serve over white rice.

Pan-Roasted Oyster-Stuffed Quail with Red-Eye Gravy
Serves 4.

> 4 quail
> 1 teaspoon Everyday Seasoning (see page 159)
> 1 quart shucked oysters
> 1 cup cornmeal
> 4 strips bacon
> 2 cups brewed coffee
> 2 tablespoons butter
> 1 tablespoon flour
> salt and pepper to taste

Season the inside of the quail with the seasoning mix. Dredge the oysters in the cornmeal. Stuff the cavities of the quail with 3 or 4 oysters each. Wrap each quail with bacon. Place in a shallow roasting pan with a rack and roast at 375 degrees for about 20 minutes.

Remove the quail and the rack from the roasting pan. Place the roasting pan on the stove and turn up the flame on medium. Pour brewed coffee into the pan and allow to boil. Reduce the heat, stirring constantly. Mash the butter and flour together until well combined, then whisk into the coffee. Stir until the butter has melted and the sauce is smooth. Adjust the seasoning with salt and pepper.

Serving suggestion: Ladle the quail with gravy and serve over Creamy Grits (see page 116) topped with crumbled blue cheese.

V. V.'s Mamma's Meatloaf with Wild Mushroom Gravy
Serves 6 to 8.

Vivián comes from a big family with six children. *How to feed them on a budget? Meatloaf! But more than an economical meal, this one is downright tasty. Hats off to Mrs. J.!*

V. V.'s Mamma's Meatloaf

4 eggs, beaten
¼ cup ketchup
¼ cup Worcestershire sauce
2 cups crushed cornflakes
1 cup panko breadcrumbs
2½ pounds ground beef
1¾ cups diced green pepper
1¾ cups diced yellow onion
1 tablespoon oregano
2 teaspoons salt
2 teaspoons pepper
1½ teaspoons dried thyme
1 tablespoon granulated garlic

In a large bowl, combine the beaten eggs, ketchup, Worcestershire sauce, cornflakes, and breadcrumbs. Allow to sit for 3 to 4 minutes to sufficiently moisten the cornflakes and breadcrumbs. Add the remaining ingredients and thoroughly combine. Turn the mixture onto a sheet tray and form into 2 loaves. Bake at 350 degrees for 45 to 50 minutes until an instant-read thermometer inserted in the center registers 160 degrees. Serve with Wild Mushroom Gravy (recipe is on the next page).

Wild Mushroom Gravy

½ cup butter
¾ cup flour
2 teaspoons chopped garlic
1½ teaspoons dried oregano
1½ tablespoons dried thyme
2 cups sliced wild mushrooms (combination of shiitake, oyster, porta-
    bella, etc.)
¾ cup julienned onion
3 tablespoons vegetable oil
4 cups Beef Stock (see page 48)
pepper to taste

Combine the butter and flour in a skillet. Slowly cook the roux about 15 minutes until brown. In a medium saucepan, combine all the remaining ingredients except the oil, Beef Stock, and pepper. Sauté in oil until soft. Add Beef Stock and bring to a boil. Add cooled roux and cook till flour taste is gone. Season with pepper. If the gravy is too thick, thin with water or additional Beef Stock and readjust seasoning.

Slow Cooker Chocolate Stout Pot Roast
Serves 6.

2½- to 3-pound beef chuck roast
2 tablespoons vegetable oil
salt and pepper to taste
2 celery stalks, chopped large
2 carrots, peeled and chopped large
1 onion, peeled and quartered
2 or 3 cloves garlic, peeled
2 tablespoons dried rosemary
2 tablespoons dried thyme
2 bay leaves
2 tablespoons tomato paste
1 bottle chocolate stout
4 cups Beef Stock (see page 48)

Rub the beef with oil and season all sides with salt and pepper. Brown the beef in a heavy skillet for 3 to 4 minutes on each side to form a nice crust. Place the vegetables and garlic in a crockpot. Sprinkle with the herbs and add bay leaves. Combine the tomato paste, stout, and Beef Stock. Place the meat on top of the vegetables and pour in the liquid. Cook on low for 8 to 10 hours. The meat should be melt-in-your-mouth tender. Remove the meat and strain the juices. For a thicker sauce, bring 2 cups of the liquid to a boil and whisk in a mixture of 2 tablespoons cornstarch and 2 tablespoons red wine or water.

Serving suggestion: Try this pot roast with braised root vegetables and Garlic Smashed Potatoes (see page 133).

Roasted Rack of Lamb with Mint Julep Sauce
Serves 4.

1 tablespoon kosher salt
1 tablespoon coarsely ground pepper
½ tablespoon dried thyme
½ tablespoon granulated garlic
1 teaspoon finely chopped rosemary
1 teaspoon dry mustard
2 Frenched racks of lamb
2 cloves garlic, sliced
2 tablespoons olive oil

Combine first 6 ingredients to make a dry rub. Cut slits in the meaty side of the racks and insert the sliced garlic cloves. Rub both sides of the racks with olive oil and sprinkle evenly with dry rub.

In a hot skillet, sear the racks for about 2 minutes on each side to brown. Place in a roasting pan and roast in a 400-degree oven for 15 to 18 minutes till a thermometer inserted in the racks reaches 125 degrees for medium-rare.

Slice and serve about 3 bones per person. Serve with Mint Julep Sauce (recipe is on the next page).

Mint Julep Sauce

1 teaspoon minced garlic
1 shallot, diced
2 tablespoons olive oil
¼ cup bourbon
2 cups Beef Stock (see page 48)
1 bunch mint (reserve a few sprigs for garnish)
2 tablespoons cornstarch
2 tablespoons red wine
salt and pepper to taste

In a medium saucepan, sauté the garlic and shallots in the olive oil for 30 seconds. Deglaze the pan with the bourbon and add Beef Stock and mint. Simmer for 15 minutes. In a separate bowl, combine the cornstarch and red wine. Slowly add to the sauce till thickened to preferred consistency. Add salt and pepper.

Serving suggestions: Garnish the lamb with mint sprigs and serve with Garlic Smashed Potatoes (see page 133) or roasted sweet potatoes.

Fish and Other Tales

Music is the key to setting the mood. The tone of the food is jazz. Sweet Potatoes *is* jazz.

Fish and Other Tales

Jesus fed the multitude with fish.
"Give a man a fish and he eats for a day; teach him to fish . . ."
You should have seen that fish I caught. It was *this big*!
And it's good fried, too.

Stuffed Trout

Deep-Fried Croaker with Herbed Tartar Sauce

Catfish NOLA

Gullah Shrimp and Crab Pilau

Blackened Snapper Niçoise

Salmon Cakes with Remoulade Sauce

Curried Shrimp and Grits

Scalloped Oysters

Crab Fritters

Stuffed Trout
Serves 6.

This is a great use of Sweet Potato Cornbread Stuffing *and makes an impressive "company's coming" presentation.*

6 10- to 16-ounce boneless trout, heads on
1 teaspoon salt
1 teaspoon pepper
½ teaspoon dried thyme
½ teaspoon dried sage
1 cup Sweet Potato Cornbread Stuffing (see page 127)
½ cup crabmeat
½ cup canned or freshly cooked collard greens, drained
6 strips bacon

Rinse the trout and open them on a flat surface. Combine the seasonings and season the inside of each trout. Combine the Sweet Potato Cornbread Stuffing, crabmeat, and greens in a small bowl. Stuff each trout with about ⅓ cup of stuffing. Fold the trout closed and wrap each with a strip of bacon. Spray a sheet tray or a shallow roasting pan large enough to hold the trout in a single layer and bake at 450 degrees for 10 minutes. Check and carefully turn the trout. Continue baking for an additional 15 minutes or until an instant-read thermometer inserted into the thickest part of the trout registers 155 degrees and the bacon is crisp.

Serving suggestion: Serve over Red Rice (see page 130) or Creamy Grits (see page 116).

Deep-Fried Croaker with Herbed Tartar Sauce
Serves 6.

I like croaker. I especially like serving it with fried okra, because it gives me the chance to call it my "Croakra Platter." But that's just me.

6 pan-dressed croaker
2 cups buttermilk
vegetable oil for frying
½ cup flour
¼ cup cornmeal
¼ cup cornstarch
1 teaspoon salt
1 teaspoon pepper
¼ teaspoon chopped garlic
¼ teaspoon dried thyme

In a bowl, cover the croaker with buttermilk. Refrigerate for 1 hour.

Fill a cast-iron Dutch oven halfway with oil and heat to 325 degrees. Mix together the flour, cornmeal, cornstarch, salt, pepper, garlic, and thyme. Dredge the fish in the flour, shaking off the excess. Place the croaker in the hot oil and fry in batches for about 10 to 12 minutes until the fish are golden brown and crispy. Serve with Herbed Tartar Sauce (recipe below).

Herbed Tartar Sauce

2 cups mayonnaise
2 tablespoons pickle relish
1 tablespoon capers
2¼ teaspoons chopped fresh parsley
1½ teaspoons dried dill
1½ teaspoons dried oregano
1½ teaspoons dried basil
3¾ teaspoons dried tarragon

1½ teaspoons chopped garlic
2 anchovies, minced, plus ¼ teaspoon anchovy oil
1 teaspoon Worcestershire sauce

Combine all the ingredients in a mixing bowl. Refrigerate.

Catfish NOLA
Serves 6.

This is pan-fried catfish deliciousness. But you can use any firm fish fillet, such as a whiting or flounder.

1 cup cornmeal
¼ cup cornstarch
½ cup flour
1 teaspoon salt
1 teaspoon pepper
½ teaspoon thyme
½ teaspoon granulated garlic
1 teaspoon paprika
pinch of cayenne pepper
6 good-sized catfish fillets
vegetable oil for frying

In a bowl or a shallow pan, combine the cornmeal, cornstarch, flour, salt, pepper, thyme, garlic, paprika, and cayenne pepper. Dredge the catfish in the mixture, shaking off any excess. In a heavy skillet or a cast-iron pan, place enough oil to come ¼ of the way up the pan. Heat the oil and add the fillets (in batches if necessary). Cook about 3 minutes on each side until they are golden brown and done. Remove the fillets and allow to drain on a rack or a plate covered with a paper towel. Serve the catfish over rice or Creamy Grits (see page 116) and top with Creole Sauce (recipe on the next page).

Creole Sauce

½ cup julienned green pepper
½ cup julienned red pepper
½ cup julienned yellow onion
¼ cup vegetable oil
1 tablespoon dried thyme
1 teaspoon Creole/Blackening Seasoning (see page 160)
1 teaspoon chopped garlic
3 ounces tomato paste
2 14.5-ounce cans diced tomatoes
2 cups water
salt and pepper to taste
Texas Pete to taste

In a medium pot, sauté the green peppers, red peppers, and on-ions in oil for about 5 minutes until the onions are translucent. Add the thyme, Creole/Blackening Seasoning, and garlic and sauté 2 to 3 minutes more. Add the tomato paste, tomatoes, and water to the pot and simmer for 20 minutes. Adjust seasonings with salt, pepper, and Texas Pete.

Gullah Shrimp and Crab Pilau
Serves 4 or 5.

This is a one-pot meal.

4 strips bacon
1 cup julienned onion
1 cup julienned green pepper
1 teaspoon Chicken and Seafood Seasoning (see page 159)
1 cup diced tomato
1 cup uncooked long-grain rice
1 tablespoon parsley, plus some for garnish
1 tablespoon Worcestershire sauce
2 cups chicken stock or water
½ cup crabmeat, picked
1 pound raw shrimp, 21 to 25 count

In a Dutch oven with a tight-fitting lid, cook the bacon until crisp. Remove the bacon, set aside to drain, and crumble. Pour off all the fat except 3 tablespoons or enough to cover the bottom of the pan. Add the onions and peppers and cook over medium-low heat until the onions are translucent. Add the Chicken and Seafood Seasoning, tomatoes, rice, parsley, Worcestershire sauce, chicken stock or water, and ½ of the crabmeat. Cook for approximately 25 minutes in a preheated 375-degree oven. Remove the pan from the oven, add the shrimp, top with the remaining crabmeat, and cook for an additional 15 minutes. Remove and garnish with parsley and crumbled reserved bacon.

Blackened Snapper Niçoise
Serves 3 or 4.

¼ cup olive oil
2 teaspoons Creole/Blackening Seasoning (see page 160)
2 tablespoons lemon juice
3- to 4-pound whole snapper, scaled and cleaned
lemon wedges for garnish

Combine the olive oil, seasoning, and lemon juice in a small bowl. Cut 3 or 4 small slashes on either side of the fish. Place the fish in a dish and coat with the marinade inside and out. Cover and refrigerate for 1 to 2 hours.

Grill the fish over medium heat for 8 to 10 minutes. Carefully turn the fish and continue to grill an additional 8 to 10 minutes until the flesh is firm. Remove to a platter and top with Niçoise Mix (recipe below). Garnish with lemon wedges.

Niçoise Mix

1 teaspoon chopped garlic
1 tablespoon Dijon mustard
1 tablespoon lemon juice
2 tablespoons white wine vinegar
1 teaspoon dried basil
½ teaspoon sugar
1 cup extra-virgin olive oil
½ cup coarsely chopped black olives
½ cup chopped green olives
1 cup seeded and diced fresh tomatoes
2 tablespoons chopped parsley
½ teaspoon fresh dill
2 tablespoons chopped pimentos
1 tablespoon diced shallots

In a small bowl, combine the garlic, Dijon mustard, lemon juice, white wine vinegar, basil, and sugar. Slowly whisk in the olive oil. In a separate bowl, combine the remaining ingredients. Pour the vinaigrette over the vegetables. Allow to sit at room temperature until ready to serve.

Salmon Cakes with Remoulade Sauce
Makes 6 Salmon Cakes.

1 pound cooked salmon
½ cup diced red pepper
½ cup diced green pepper
¼ cup chopped green onions
2 cups panko breadcrumbs
4 eggs, lightly beaten
1 tablespoon basil
2 tablespoons mayonnaise
1 tablespoon Dijon mustard
1 tablespoon dried dill
1 tablespoon granulated garlic
salt and pepper to taste
6 hamburger or Kaiser rolls, sliced and toasted

Combine all the ingredients except the rolls and divide into 6 patties. Place the patties in a skillet or a grill pan and cook over medium heat for about 5 minutes per side. Place on the toasted rolls and top with Remoulade Sauce (recipe below).

Remoulade Sauce
Makes about 2 cups.

1 cup mayonnaise
1 bunch green onions, thinly sliced
2 tablespoons Creole mustard
1 tablespoon chopped parsley
1 teaspoon chopped garlic
2 teaspoons horseradish
1 cup cooked salad shrimp
2 teaspoons Creole/Blackening Seasoning (see page 160)
2 or 3 shakes Texas Pete

Combine all the ingredients and refrigerate.

Curried Shrimp and Grits
Serves 8.

3 cups water
1 teaspoon salt
1 pound salad shrimp
½ cup diced green pepper
½ cup diced red pepper
¼ cup diced yellow onion
¼ cup vegetable oil
1 tablespoon curry powder
¼ cup flour
¼ cup diced tomato
¼ cup coconut milk

Bring the water and salt to a boil in a pot. Add the shrimp and cook about 5 to 7 minutes until pink. Strain the shrimp and reserve the shrimp stock. In the same pot, add the vegetables and oil and sauté until the vegetables are a little soft. Add the curry powder and cook about 1 minute until the curry powder is fragrant. Add the flour and stir to combine. Slowly add 2 cups of the reserved shrimp stock, stirring continuously. Simmer for about 5 minutes. Add the shrimp, tomatoes, and coconut milk. Return to a simmer and cook until heated through. Serve over Creamy Grits (recipe below).

Creamy Grits

4 cups heavy cream
½ cup butter
1 tablespoon salt ½ salt
1 cup stone-ground grits

In a heavy-bottomed saucepan, bring the heavy cream, butter, and salt to a slow boil. Whisk in the grits and reduce the heat to low. Cook, stirring frequently, about 45 to 50 minutes until the grits are thick and tender.

Scalloped Oysters
Serves 6.

This is a very elegant and simple presentation.

1 quart shucked oysters
¼ teaspoon salt
¼ teaspoon pepper
pinch of cayenne pepper
¼ cup lemon juice
½ cup butter, cut into small cubes
1 quart cracker crumbs or toasted Sweet Potato Biscuit crumbs (see
    page 138)
1 cup heavy cream
¼ cup grated Parmesan cheese

Preheat oven to 400 degrees. Place a layer of oysters in each of six 4-ounce ovenproof ramekins. Season with the salt, pepper, and cayenne pepper. Sprinkle with lemon juice. Dot each ramekin with butter. Top with the cracker crumbs or Sweet Potato Biscuit crumbs. Repeat with 2 or more layers, ending with the crumbs. Pour the heavy cream over each, using just enough to moisten. Top with the Parmesan cheese. Place the ramekins on a sheet tray and bake for 15 to 20 minutes until heated through and until the tops are brown.

Crab Fritters
Serves 6 or 7.

1 cup biscuit mix
1 teaspoon Chicken and Seafood Seasoning (see page 159)
¼ teaspoon cayenne pepper
½ teaspoon lemon zest
1 tablespoon chopped parsley
1 egg, lightly beaten
¼ cup buttermilk
¼ teaspoon Worcestershire sauce
½ cup corn
½ pound crabmeat
vegetable oil for frying

Combine the biscuit mix, seasoning, cayenne pepper, lemon zest, and parsley. In a separate bowl, mix the lightly beaten egg, buttermilk, and Worcestershire sauce. Add to the dry ingredients. Fold in the corn and crabmeat. Heat a skillet filled halfway with oil. Drop fritters by the spoonful into the oil. Fry for about 2 to 3 minutes until the fritters are golden and crispy. Remove and drain on paper towels. Serve with Herbed Tartar Sauce (see page 108).

Side Dishes and Stuff

Friends have been made
and relationships forged over
a basket of Fried Green Tomatoes and Okra.

Side Dishes and Stuff

The problem is sometimes what to prepare to go along with the main course. Not so in the South. At Thanksgiving or at Sunday dinner, sometimes we'd have all of the following and a few more. That's a little extreme, but oddly enough no one ever complained.

Three-Cheese Macaroni and Country Ham Soufflé

Spicy Greens

Candied Sweet Potatoes

Sweet Potato Cornbread

Crackling Cornbread

Sweet Potato Cornbread Stuffing

Okra, Corn, and Tomatoes

Fried Green Tomatoes and Okra

Confetti Rice

Red Rice

Plain White Rice

Sweet Potato, Corn, and Country Ham Risotto

Mashed Sweet Potatoes

Garlic Smashed Potatoes

Three-Cheese Macaroni and Country Ham Soufflé
Serves 10 to 12.

*This should be a food group **all by itself!***

16-ounce package macaroni
3 cups shredded sharp yellow cheddar cheese, plus additional for
    topping
2 cups crumbled blue cheese
¼ cup shredded Parmesan cheese
10 eggs, lightly beaten
1 cup sour cream
1 cup heavy cream
2 tablespoons dried dill
½ teaspoon white pepper
1 pound country ham, chopped
¼ cup butter or bacon grease

Cook the macaroni accordingly to the package directions. Drain and place in a large bowl. While the macaroni is still hot, add the cheeses. Mix until the cheeses are melted. In a separate bowl, combine the lightly beaten eggs, sour cream, heavy cream, dill, and white pepper. Thoroughly combine the egg mixture with the macaroni mixture. Sauté the ham in butter or bacon grease about 2 minutes until the ham is just done. Add to the egg mixture. Spray a 4-quart baking dish. Pour the mixture into the dish and top with additional cheese. Bake at 375 degrees for 20 to 25 minutes until the soufflé has set and the cheese is bubbling and starting to brown.

Spicy Greens
Serves 10 to 12.

This dish can be as spicy as you like. If you are faint of heart (burn), eliminate the red pepper altogether. Either way, don't forget the cornbread!

8 quarts chicken stock or water
1 or 2 pieces smoked turkey necks or legs
1 tablespoon dried thyme
4 or 5 cloves garlic, peeled
¾ teaspoon red pepper flakes
1 tablespoon salt
1 onion, chopped
3 bunches collard greens, cleaned
1 bunch mustard greens, cleaned
2 bunches turnip greens, cleaned
¼ pound butter
¼ cup cider vinegar
1 tablespoon sugar

Boil the chicken stock or water in a large pot. Add the smoked turkey, thyme, garlic, red pepper flakes, salt, and onions. Reduce the temperature and simmer for about ½ hour to sufficiently season liquid. Add the greens and return to a boil. Reduce to a simmer and cook about 1 hour until the greens are tender. Remove the smoked turkey. Remove the bones and return the meat to the greens. Stir in the butter, vinegar, and sugar.

Candied Sweet Potatoes
Serves 8 to 10.

5 quarts sweet potatoes, peeled and sliced ¼ inch
4½ cups sugar
1 cup brown sugar
1 teaspoon cinnamon
½ teaspoon nutmeg

1½ teaspoons vanilla extract
1½ teaspoons lemon extract
1 cup butter, cubed

In a large baking pan or a casserole dish, place a layer of sweet potatoes. In a medium bowl, combine the sugar, brown sugar, cinnamon, and nutmeg. Cover the layer of sweet potatoes with ¼ of the sugar mixture. Sprinkle a little of the vanilla and lemon extracts over the mixture. Dot the layer with ¼ of the butter cubes. Repeat layers until the potatoes, sugar mixture, extracts, and butter are used. Cover the pan with aluminum foil and bake at 375 degrees for 1½ hours or until the potatoes are tender. Remove the foil and drain ½ of the liquid, then bake uncovered for an additional ½ hour to caramelize the potatoes and syrup.

Sweet Potato Cornbread
Makes 12 muffins or one 9-inch pan.

Nothing is better than cornbread and greens—except Sweet Potato Cornbread and greens! This cornbread is also the base of great stuffing (or dressing).

¾ cup all-purpose flour
1¼ cups yellow cornmeal
1 tablespoon baking powder
1 teaspoon salt
½ cup sugar
½ teaspoon cinnamon
½ teaspoon nutmeg
2 eggs, lightly beaten
2 tablespoons vegetable oil
1¼ cups milk
½ cup mashed sweet potatoes

In a large bowl, loosely sift the dry ingredients. In a separate bowl, combine the lightly beaten eggs, oil, and milk. Add the sweet potatoes and mix well. Add the sweet potato mixture to the dry ingredients and combine, being careful not to overmix. Pour into a greased 9-inch baking pan or spoon into a 12-cup muffin tin. Bake at 450 degrees for 20 minutes until the cornbread is golden.

Crackling Cornbread
Serves 6 to 8.

This is definitely high-test cornbread. Cracklings are deep-fried crispy skins of various animals—in this case, pork.

2 tablespoons bacon grease
1½ cups white cornmeal
½ cup flour
1½ teaspoons baking powder
½ teaspoon baking soda
1 teaspoon salt
1 teaspoon sugar
1 cup pork cracklings
½ cup finely diced onion
1¼ cups buttermilk
4 eggs, lightly beaten
3 tablespoons vegetable oil (bacon grease may be substituted)

Place the 2 tablespoons bacon grease in a 10-inch cast-iron skillet. Put the skillet in a 400-degree oven to heat up. In a mixing bowl, combine the cornmeal, flour, baking powder, baking soda, salt, and sugar. Add the cracklings and onions. Combine the buttermilk, lightly beaten eggs, and oil and mix thoroughly into the dry ingredients. Remove the skillet from the oven and pour the batter into the hot skillet. Return the skillet to the oven and bake for 20 to 25 minutes until the cornbread is firm and golden brown. Cut into wedges.

Sweet Potato Cornbread Stuffing
Serves 8 to 10.

This pairs well with fish, poultry, or pork. It will definitely make that turkey glad he took one for the cause!

¼ cup butter
2 cups diced onion
2 cups diced green pepper
1 cup diced celery
2 tablespoons rubbed sage
1 tablespoon dried thyme
½ teaspoon red pepper flakes
3½ quarts (double batch) toasted **Sweet Potato Cornbread** crumbs (see pages 125–26)
chopped green onions, green part only
1 cup chopped parsley
1 cup chicken stock or water
2 eggs, lightly beaten

In a large skillet, melt the butter and sauté the onions, peppers, celery, and seasonings until the vegetables are soft. Remove from heat and allow to cool. In a large mixing bowl, add the toasted cornbread, green onions, and parsley. Add the sautéed vegetables and combine well. Moisten with the chicken stock or water and add the lightly beaten eggs. Place the stuffing in a buttered casserole dish and bake at 375 degrees for 25 minutes or until it is light brown on top and heated through.

Okra, Corn, and Tomatoes
Serves 4 to 6.

On lazy days, this is a great entrée served over white rice. Okra gets slimy. The addition of onions and the acidic tomatoes makes it less slimy.

4 strips bacon
¼ cup diced onion
¼ cup diced celery
¼ cup diced green pepper
1 teaspoon Creole/Blackening Seasoning (see page 160)
1 teaspoon chopped garlic
2 cups sliced fresh or frozen okra
3 ears fresh corn, removed from cobs, or 2 cups frozen corn
1 cup water or chicken stock
1½ cups diced tomatoes

In a medium pot, cook the bacon until crisp. Reserve and crumble the bacon. Add the onions, celery, green peppers, and seasoning and sauté in the bacon fat until the onions are soft. Add the garlic and sauté 1 more minute. Add the okra, corn, and water or chicken stock. Cover and cook for 10 minutes or until the okra is tender. Add the diced tomatoes and cook for 2 to 3 minutes until the tomatoes are heated through. Top with the reserved crumbled bacon. Serve as a side or over white rice as a light main course.

Fried Green Tomatoes and Okra
Serves 6.

1 cup all-purpose flour
2 cups yellow cornmeal
2 tablespoons cornstarch
1 tablespoon Everyday Seasoning (see page 159)
2 cups buttermilk
4 good-sized green tomatoes, sliced

½ pound fresh okra, tips removed, cut into ½-inch slices
vegetable oil for frying

In a medium bowl, combine the flour, cornmeal, cornstarch, and Everyday Seasoning. Pour the buttermilk into a separate bowl. Dip the tomatoes in the buttermilk, then dredge them in the flour and cornmeal mix. Place on a sheet tray. Repeat with the okra. Place the vegetables in the freezer for about 20 minutes.

Pour oil halfway up a large skillet. Remove the vegetables from the freezer. When the oil is hot, put the tomatoes in the oil in a single layer. Fry about 3 minutes till brown. Turn and brown the other side. Fry in batches if necessary. Remove to a plate covered with a paper towel to drain. Add the okra in a single layer and fry 3 to 4 minutes until golden brown. Remove and drain.

Don't forget a big bottle of Texas Pete!

Confetti Rice

Serves 4.

Confetti Rice is pretty and colorful.

2 cups water
1 tablespoon butter
½ teaspoon salt
1 cup rice
2 tablespoons vegetable oil
½ cup combination of diced green, red, and yellow peppers
½ cup diced onion
¼ cup diced celery
6 ounces frozen mixed vegetables
¼ cup chopped fresh herbs (parsley, dill, basil, etc.)

In a medium pot, bring the water, butter, and salt to a boil. Add the rice and return to a boil. Reduce to a simmer and cook covered for 20 minutes. Add the oil to a sauté pan and cook the peppers, onions, and celery for about 5 minutes until the onions are soft. Add the sautéed vegetables to the pot of rice. Add the frozen vegetables as well. Return the lid and let sit for 10 minutes. Mix in the fresh herbs.

Red Rice

Serves 6 to 8.

Vivián's family is from Bluffton, South Carolina—Gullah country. I have yet to go to a function there that did not include Red Rice. Delicious.

2 slices bacon
2 tablespoons vegetable oil
½ cup diced onion
¼ cup diced celery
¼ cup diced green pepper
½ cup diced smoked sausage

1 teaspoon Chicken and Seafood Seasoning (see page 159)
6 ounces tomato sauce
3 cups water
2 cups rice
2 green onions, chopped, green part only

In a Dutch oven, cook the bacon till crispy. Remove to the side and crumble. Add the vegetable oil, onions, celery, and peppers. Cook about 3 to 4 minutes till soft. Add the smoked sausage and cook 2 minutes more. Add the seasoning, tomato sauce, and water. Bring to a boil and add the rice. Cover and reduce to a simmer. Cook for 25 minutes until the rice is tender and all the liquid has been absorbed. Let sit for about 10 minutes. Remove the lid and stir in the reserved crumbled bacon and green onions.

Plain White Rice
Serves 4.

Vivián doesn't know how to make rice. Could there be others?

2 cups water
2 tablespoons butter
1 teaspoon salt
1 bay leaf
1 cup long-grain rice

In a saucepan, bring the water, butter, salt, and bay leaf to a boil. Add the rice and return the pot to a boil. Lower the heat and simmer covered for 15 to 20 minutes. Turn off the heat and let sit for 10 minutes. Uncover and fluff the rice with a fork. Remove the bay leaf.

Sweet Potato, Corn, and Country Ham Risotto
Serves 4.

This Italian-style short-grain rice dish gets a slight drawl with the addition of country ham and sweet potatoes.

2 teaspoons finely diced onion
¼ cup diced country ham
½ cup peeled and diced sweet potato
1½ teaspoons dried basil
¼ cup vegetable oil
1 teaspoon chopped garlic
1 cup Arborio rice
3 cups hot chicken stock
½ cup canned or frozen corn
2 tablespoons butter
2 tablespoons grated Parmesan cheese
¼ cup finely sliced green onions

In a medium pot, sauté the onions, country ham, sweet potatoes, and basil in the oil about 5 to 6 minutes until the onions and ham are fragrant and the sweet potatoes start to soften. Add the garlic and cook 1 minute more. Add the rice and cook, stirring, about 1 minute until the rice is coated and toasty. Add ⅓ of the hot stock and cook, stirring constantly, until most of the liquid is absorbed. Repeat with another ⅓ of the stock. Add the remaining stock along with the corn and continue cooking until the liquid is absorbed. Finish the risotto with the butter and Parmesan cheese. Garnish with the green onions.

Mashed Sweet Potatoes
Serves 4 to 6.

Baking the potatoes instead of peeling and boiling them extracts more flavor.

4 or 5 sweet potatoes
¼ cup butter
¼ cup heavy cream
1½ teaspoons salt
½ teaspoon granulated garlic
1½ teaspoons vanilla extract
½ cup firmly packed brown sugar

Rinse the sweet potatoes and wrap them in aluminum foil. Place the potatoes on a sheet tray and bake in a 375-degree oven for about 45 minutes until soft. Allow the potatoes to cool.

Peel the potatoes and purée in batches in a food processor. In a medium saucepan, add all the ingredients except the potatoes. Bring to a simmer and add the potatoes. Stir to thoroughly combine and heat through.

Garlic Smashed Potatoes
Serves 4 to 6.

2 teaspoons kosher salt
2 pounds red new potatoes
4 cloves garlic, peeled
3 tablespoons butter
½ cup half-and-half
pepper to taste

In a medium pot, add the salt, potatoes, garlic cloves, and enough water to cover the potatoes by 4 inches. Bring to a boil. Lower the heat to a simmer and cook until the potatoes and garlic are soft. Remove from heat and drain in a colander. Return the potatoes to the pot. Smash the potatoes with a masher or a sturdy whip. Blend in the butter. Heat the half-and-half in a small pot, then stir it in with the potatoes a little at a time until potatoes reach desired consistency. Season with pepper.

A
Sweet
Potatoes
Brunch

Food is king, but good service is his queen.

A Sweet Potatoes Brunch

I must say, I approached brunch at Sweet Potatoes kicking and screaming—*never*!!! Sunday was my one day off. Yet Vivian in her calm but insistent manner talked me into it. It has become one of my favorite things to do. It's the food and, of course, the beverages.

Sweet Potato Biscuits

Trade Street Benedict

Eggs Sardou

Creole Frittata

Egg Salad and Crab Club

Sweet Potato Pancakes with Apple Marmalade
and Honey-Ginger Butter

Sausage Gravy

Autumn Fruit Bowl

Eye-Openers

Bloody Ginny

Vivian's Mimosa

Sweet Potato Dash

Sweet Potato Fantasy

Mojito

Mint Julep

Mint Iced Tea

Sweet Potato Biscuits
Makes about 18 biscuits.

These are a versatile favorite. They are worth making just to have the leftovers so you can create things to do with them!

2 cups plain flour (such as White Lily)
¼ teaspoon baking soda
3 teaspoons baking powder
2 tablespoons sugar
¼ teaspoon cinnamon
¼ teaspoon nutmeg
pinch of ground cloves
½ teaspoon salt
½ cup shortening, chilled
¼ cup butter, chilled and cubed
¾ cup buttermilk
1 baked sweet potato, peeled and mashed
melted butter

In a medium mixing bowl, sift together the flour, baking soda, baking powder, sugar, cinnamon, nutmeg, cloves, and salt. Cut in the shortening and butter with a fork until the mixture resembles coarse meal. In a separate bowl, combine the buttermilk and mashed sweet potato. Add this to the flour mixture and stir until combined. The dough will be very wet. Turn the dough onto a well-floured surface. Knead the dough until it starts to come together. Roll the dough to about ½-inch thickness. Cut the dough with a 2-inch biscuit cutter and place in a parchment-lined baking pan. For biscuits with soft sides, place the biscuits close together, almost touching. Otherwise, place them 2 inches apart. Bake at 400 degrees for 10 to 12 minutes until the biscuits are golden brown. Brush with the melted butter.

Trade Street Benedict
Serves 4 to 8.

This is our vision of the classic eggs Benedict!

2 tablespoons white vinegar
8 eggs
1 tablespoon butter
4 Sweet Potato Biscuits, split (see page 138)
8 slices country ham
1 recipe Pimento Cheese Fondue (recipe below)
bacon bits for garnish

Fill a skillet or a heavy saucepan with 2 to 3 inches of water. Add the vinegar and bring to a simmer. Carefully break the eggs into the water. Cook for about 3 minutes until the whites are firm but the yolks are still soft.

In a hot skillet or a griddle top, melt the butter and toast the biscuits. Remove the biscuits to a platter. Add the country ham to the hot skillet and cook about 1 minute on each side. Place a slice of ham on each biscuit and top each with a poached egg. Add the Pimento Cheese Fondue on top and garnish with bacon bits.

Pimento Cheese Fondue

2 tablespoons melted butter
¼ cup flour
1 cup chicken stock
2 cups heavy cream
1 bay leaf
¼ teaspoon nutmeg
¼ teaspoon white pepper
½ teaspoon ground mustard
¾ teaspoon smoked paprika
1 teaspoon granulated garlic
¼ teaspoon sugar
pinch of cayenne pepper

1½ cups shredded yellow cheddar cheese
¼ cup drained and chopped pimentos

In a medium saucepan, combine the butter and flour. Heat without browning. Slowly whisk in the stock and heavy cream. Bring to a simmer and add the bay leaf, nutmeg, white pepper, mustard, paprika, garlic, sugar, and cayenne pepper. Add the cheddar cheese. Stir until the cheese has melted. Cook for about 10 minutes until the flour taste has gone. Remove from heat and fold in the pimentos.

Eggs Sardou

Serves 4.

Eggs Sardou is a Louisiana dish usually consisting of poached eggs, creamed spinach, and hollandaise. It is named after Victorien Sardou, a famous French dramatist who visited New Orleans, where the dish was invented. I'm thinking they must have really liked this guy, and that he must have really liked eggs.

8 artichoke bottoms (13.75-ounce can artichoke bottoms)
8 poached eggs (see poaching instructions under Trade Street Benedict, page 140)
8 slices beefsteak tomato
1 cup Creamed Spinach (recipe below)
It's a Cinch! Hollandaise Sauce (recipe on next page)

Heat the artichoke bottoms in the egg poaching water for about 1 minute until hot. Place 2 slices of tomato on each of 4 plates. Top each pair of tomato slices with about ¼ cup Creamed Spinach. Place the artichoke bottoms on the Creamed Spinach and carefully place a poached egg in each artichoke bottom. Ladle each with hollandaise.

Creamed Spinach

1 pound frozen spinach
1 medium onion, diced
⅓ cup butter
¼ cup flour
3 cups heavy cream
1½ tablespoons Pernod or other licorice-flavored liqueur
⅓ cup Parmesan cheese
salt and white pepper to taste

Thaw the spinach and drain well. Sauté the onions in butter until soft. Add the flour and cook for 1 minute. Slowly stir in the heavy cream till smooth. Add the liqueur. Cook until the sauce thickens, then add the Parmesan cheese. Stir to mix. Fold in the drained spinach and heat through. Season with salt and white pepper.

It's a Cinch! Hollandaise Sauce

5 egg yolks
2 tablespoons lemon juice
zest of 1 lemon
2 teaspoons Texas Pete
1½ cups melted butter
2 teaspoons salt
½ teaspoon white pepper

In a blender or a food processor, add the egg yolks, lemon juice, zest, and Texas Pete. Blend until the yolks thicken and turn pale. Slowly add the melted butter until sauce thickens. Add the salt and white pepper.

Creole Frittata
Serves 6.

¼ cup melted butter or vegetable oil
1 cup cooked baby shrimp
1 cup diced green or red pepper
8 ounces cooked salmon
2 teaspoons Creole/Blackening Seasoning (see page 160)
12 large eggs, beaten
2 cups shredded yellow cheddar cheese
1 cup Creole Sauce (see page 110)
1 cup crabmeat

Add the melted butter or oil to a large sauté pan or a 10-inch skillet. Add the shrimp, peppers, salmon, and seasoning. Cook for 1 to 2 minutes until the ingredients are heated through and the flavors are combined. Pour the beaten eggs over the seafood and vegetables and cook about 3 minutes until eggs start to set. Sprinkle with the cheese and place under a broiler for 3 to 4 minutes until cheese is melted and eggs are set. Remove from the oven and carefully slide the frittata onto a serving plate. Cut into wedges and top with Creole Sauce and crabmeat.

Egg Salad and Crab Club
Serves 5.

10 hard-cooked eggs, peeled and chopped
¼ cup 'Tata Salad Dressing (see page 65)
4 ounces crabmeat, picked
¼ teaspoon Old Bay seasoning
10 slices hearty wheat bread, toasted
1¼ cups baby spinach
1 ripe tomato, sliced
10 strips bacon, cooked

In a medium bowl, carefully combine the chopped eggs with the 'Tata Salad Dressing, crabmeat, and Old Bay seasoning. Top ½ of the wheat toast with ¼ cup each of the baby spinach. Add 1 tomato slice each and top with ½ cup of the egg salad. Finish each sandwich with 2 strips of bacon and top with the remaining toast.

Serving suggestion: Serve with a side of apples.

Sweet Potato Pancakes with Apple Marmalade and Honey-Ginger Butter
Makes about 10 pancakes.

Sweet Potato Pancakes

1¼ cups flour
½ teaspoon salt
2 teaspoons baking powder
1 teaspoon baking soda
3 tablespoons sugar
¼ teaspoon ground cinnamon

¼ teaspoon ground nutmeg
¼ teaspoon ground ginger
2 cups buttermilk
2 eggs, beaten
¼ cup melted butter
½ teaspoon vanilla extract
¼ teaspoon lemon extract
1 cup mashed sweet potatoes

Combine the flour, salt, baking powder, baking soda, sugar, cinnamon, nutmeg, and ginger in a bowl. In a separate bowl, mix together the buttermilk, beaten eggs, butter, vanilla extract, lemon extract, and sweet potatoes. Add to the flour mixture and combine, being careful not to overmix.

Lightly grease a hot griddle. Add ⅓ cup of batter to the griddle. Cook until the pancake starts to bubble. Turn the pancake and cook until golden. Repeat until all the batter is used. Top pancakes with Apple Marmalade (recipe below) and Honey-Ginger Butter (recipe below).

Apple Marmalade

3 pounds peeled, cored, and diced apples
2 cups firmly packed brown sugar
¼ cup dark corn syrup
½ teaspoon ground cinnamon
½ teaspoon ground nutmeg
¼ teaspoon ground ginger

Place all the ingredients in a large saucepan and simmer over medium heat for 20 to 30 minutes until the apples are soft. Mash the apples with a sturdy whip or a potato masher. Serve warm.

Honey-Ginger Butter

2 sticks salted butter, softened
½ teaspoon ground ginger
3 tablespoons honey

Combine the ingredients in the bowl of an electric mixer with the whip attachment. Mix on medium until the butter is light and fluffy.

Sausage Gravy
Serves 4 to 6.

½ pound country sausage
1½ teaspoons dried sage
½ teaspoon dried thyme
pinch of red pepper flakes
¼ cup flour
2 cups milk
1 teaspoon pepper

In a large skillet, brown the sausage along with the sage, thyme, and red pepper flakes. Remove the sausage with a slotted spoon and set aside. Add the flour to the skillet and combine to make a light roux. Slowly stir in the milk and bring to a simmer. Return the sausage to the pan and continue cooking for about 10 to 15 minutes till the flour taste is gone. Season with pepper.

Serving suggestion: Spoon over a big ole toasted Sweet Potato Biscuit (see page 138) and garnish with crumbled bacon.

Autumn Fruit Bowl
Serves 6 to 8.

6 apples (Red or Golden Delicious, Honey Crisp, or a combination)
3 Bartlett pears
1 teaspoon lemon juice
1 cup dried cranberries
½ teaspoon ground cinnamon
½ teaspoon ground nutmeg
⅓ cup honey

Core and dice the apples and pears and place them in a mixing bowl. Toss with the lemon juice to help prevent the fruit from turning brown. Add the cranberries and the remaining ingredients and mix well.

Eye-Openers

It's Sunday morning **until 12:01.** *Then it's time for a Sweet Potatoes Eye-Opener.*

Bloody Ginny
Serves 1.

1¾ ounces Hendrick's gin (or your favorite brand)
¼ ounce dry vermouth
4 ounces Bloody Mary mix (a local favorite is F&TJ's)
3 olives for garnish
pickled okra for garnish

Fill a mixing cup with ice. Add the gin, dry vermouth, and Bloody Mary mix. Stir (don't shake!) and pour into a large stemmed glass. Garnish with the olives and a spear of pickled okra.

Vivián's Mimosa
Serves 4 to 6.

Let's be festive and make a pitcher!

3 splits chilled champagne
16 ounces ice-cold orange juice
4 ounces Grand Marnier or other orange-flavored liqueur
½ orange slices for garnish

Fill a chilled pitcher with champagne, orange juice, and Grand Marnier. Pour into champagne flutes and garnish with ½ orange slices.

Sweet Potato Dash
Serves 1.

1½ ounces Jack Daniel's whiskey
½ ounce amaretto
2 ounces sour mix
2 ounces pineapple juice

Pour the ingredients over ice in your favorite rock glass. Adjust the amounts to fit your day.

Sweet Potato Fantasy
Serves 1.

1 ounce Grey Goose vodka
¾ ounce black raspberry liqueur
1 ounce orange juice
2½ ounces champagne

Use a mixing cup to combine vodka, black raspberry liqueur, and orange juice. Shake well. Pour into a chilled 9-ounce martini glass and top with champagne.

Mojito
Serves 1.

1 ounce lite rum
1½ ounces spiced rum
2 ounces Mint Simple Syrup (recipe below)
3 lime wedges
1 ounce club soda
3 mint leaves

In a Collins glass, combine over ice the lite rum, spiced rum, Mint Simple Syrup, and juice squeezed from the lime wedges. Top with the club soda and garnish with the mint leaves.

Mint Simple Syrup

3 cups sugar
½ teaspoon lemon juice
2 cups water
2 cups mint leaves, including stems

Add the sugar, lemon juice, and water to a medium pot. Tear the mint leaves and stems and add them to the pot. Cook on medium-high heat until the sugar dissolves, then turn down the heat and simmer for 10 to 15 minutes. Strain and store in the refrigerator.

Mint Julep

Serves 1.

My personal favorite.

2 ounces Mint Simple Syrup (see page 152)
1½ ounces Maker's Mark bourbon
4 ounces lemon-lime soda

Pour the ingredients over ice in a Collins glass.

Mint Iced Tea

Serves 6 to 8.

½ gallon boiling water
6 large iced-tea bags
2 cups Mint Simple Syrup (see page 152)
small bunch of mint for garnish

Using a heat-resistant pitcher, pour the boiling water over the tea bags and let steep for about 10 minutes. Remove the tea bags. Add the Mint Simple Syrup to desired sweetness. Serve over ice with the mint leaves as garnish.

A Little Bit of This and a Little Bit of That

Good friends, good conversation, and great food—
an extension of our living room

A Little Bit of This and a Little Bit of That

My grandmother probably had only four or five seasonings that she used in her cooking: salt, black pepper, and lemon and vanilla extracts and nutmeg for desserts. Still, everything was perfectly seasoned and memorable. I, on the other hand, am a sauce-and-spice junkie. I love blending herbs and spices and creating sauces not to hide but to enhance flavors. My grandmother is an example of how you don't need a lot of herbs, spices, and such to make food delicious; you just have to have no fear in using them.

Below are a few seasonings, toppings, and condiments for everyday use. The lovely people in the Louisiana area have a term that applies here—lagniappe, or "a little extra."

Everyday Seasoning

Chicken and Seafood Seasoning

Steak Seasoning

Creole/Blackening Seasoning

Chili Sauce

Strawberry Compote

Molasses Dijon Dressing

Cranberry Vinaigrette

Blue Cheese Dressing

1000 Island Dressing

Everyday Seasoning
Makes 2 cups.

1 cup kosher salt
½ cup pepper
¼ cup granulated garlic
¼ cup dried thyme

Combine all the ingredients and store in an airtight container.

Chicken and Seafood Seasoning
Makes about 1 cup.

This is the base for many of the seasoning blends we use in the restaurant. It is very useful for some of the recipes in this book.

6 tablespoons kosher salt
6 tablespoons coarsely ground pepper
3 tablespoons granulated garlic
1 tablespoon dried thyme
1 tablespoon dried mustard
1 tablespoon smoked paprika
1½ tablespoons ground nutmeg

Combine all the ingredients and store in an airtight container.

Steak Seasoning
Makes 2 cups.

1 cup Chicken and Seafood Seasoning (see above)
½ cup brown sugar
½ cup dry coffee

Combine all the ingredients and store in an airtight container.

Creole/Blackening Seasoning
Makes ¾ cup.

½ cup Chicken and Seafood Seasoning (see page 159)
1½ teaspoons chili powder
1½ teaspoons onion powder
¾ teaspoon cayenne pepper, or to taste
½ teaspoon pepper
¼ teaspoon white pepper
1½ tablespoons dried oregano
1 teaspoon sugar

Combine all the ingredients and store in an airtight container.

Chili Sauce
Makes about 4 cups.

This is great for hot dogs as well as hamburgers.

1 pound ground beef
1 small onion, diced
1 teaspoon granulated garlic
1½ tablespoons chili powder
1 tablespoon cumin
2 tablespoons Texas Pete
¼ cup ketchup
1 cube beef bouillon
½ cup water
1 tablespoon soy sauce
2 tablespoons tomato paste

Brown the hamburger in a skillet or a saucepan. Add the onions, garlic, chili powder, and cumin and cook until the onions are soft. Add the hot sauce and ketchup. Dissolve the bouillon cube in the water. Add the bouillon, soy sauce, and tomato paste to the skillet. Cook on low heat for about 10 minutes until thick.

Strawberry Compote
Makes 4 cups.

1 quart strawberries, hulled and quartered
1 cup sugar
¼ cup corn syrup
1 tablespoon orange liqueur

Bring all the ingredients to a simmer in a small saucepan. Cook on low for about 25 to 30 minutes until sauce thickens.

Serving suggestion: This is great as a topping for Sweet Potato Biscuits (see page 138) or Sour Cream Pound Cake (see page 37).

Molasses Dijon Dressing
Makes about 3 cups.

We started with Honey Mustard Dressing on our menu. One day, I ran out of honey, but I needed the dressing. I substituted molasses for the honey. I like it better. It adds a lot more flavor. Try it on a Sweet Potato Biscuit (see page138) with country ham.

2 cups Dijon mustard
¼ cup mayonnaise
½ cup molasses
pinch of cayenne pepper

In a small mixing bowl, combine the mustard and mayonnaise. Add the molasses and cayenne pepper and stir until smooth. Cover and refrigerate.

Cranberry Vinaigrette
Makes 4 cups.

1 cup Dijon mustard
½ cup apple cider vinegar
½ cup whole cranberry sauce
2 cups olive oil
pepper to taste

Combine the mustard, vinegar, and cranberry sauce in a food processor. Blend while slowly adding the oil. Season with pepper.

Blue Cheese Dressing
Makes about 1 quart.

This is also a great dip for vegetables and chips. It's a definite plus as an accompaniment for spicy wings.

2 cups mayonnaise
1 cup sour cream
½ cup milk
1 tablespoon onion powder
1 tablespoon dried dill
1 tablespoon granulated garlic
1 tablespoon Worcestershire sauce
½ teaspoon salt
½ teaspoon white pepper
1½ cups crumbled blue cheese

In a mixing bowl, combine all the ingredients except for the blue cheese crumbles. Mix well. Add the blue cheese. Adjust thickness by adding more milk.

1000 Island Dressing
Makes 3½ cups.

Maybe we should call it 10,000 Island Dressing because it's extra good!

2 cups mayonnaise
¼ cup bottled chili sauce
½ cup jalapeño chow chow
1½ cups diced onion
3 hard-cooked eggs, chopped
1½ teaspoons chopped parsley
1 tablespoon chili powder
1 tablespoon dried tarragon

Combine all the ingredients in a mixing bowl. Blend until smooth. Cover and refrigerate.

Index

WELL, SHUT MY MOUTH!